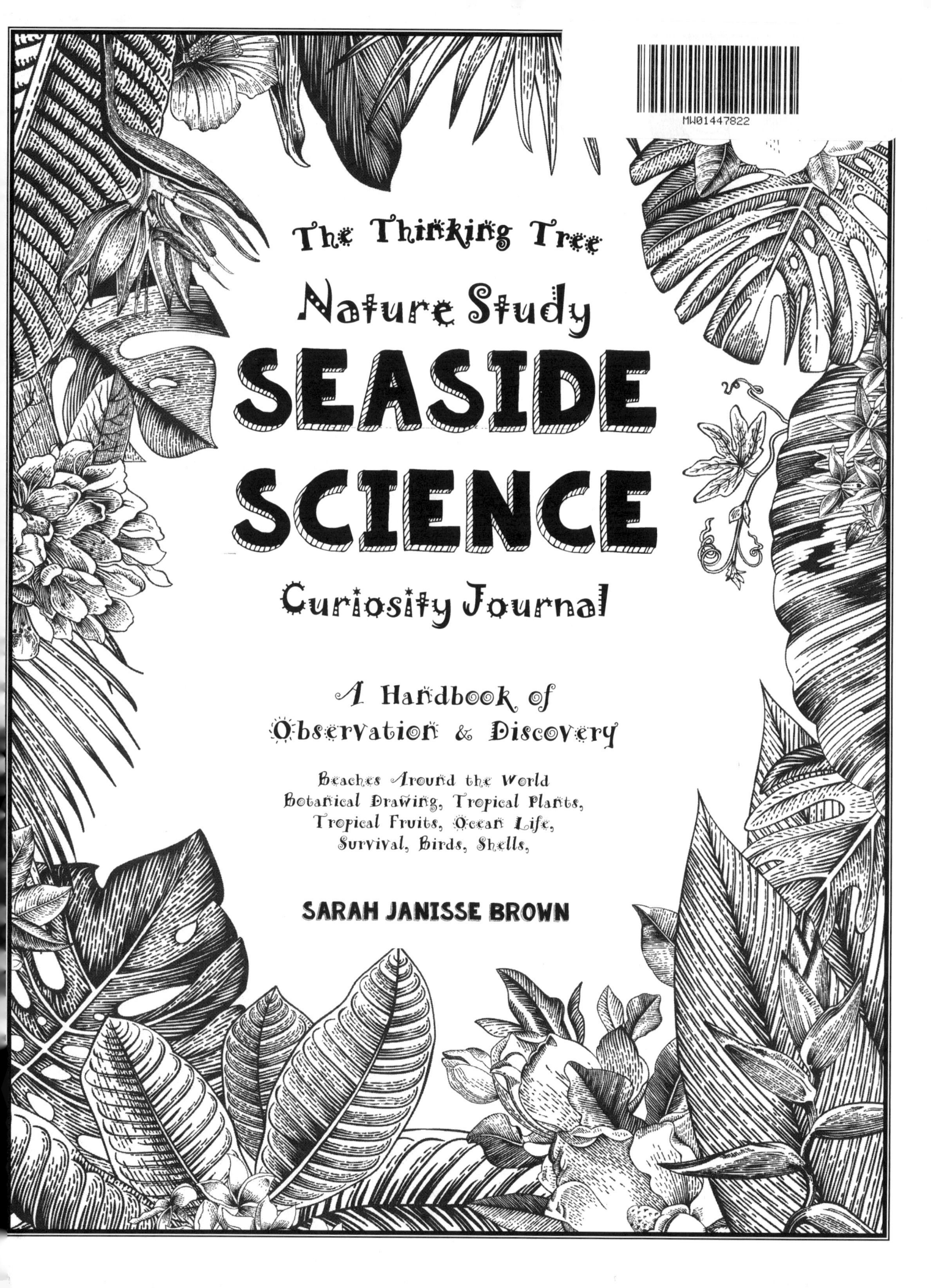

The Thinking Tree
Nature Study
SEASIDE SCIENCE
Curiosity Journal

A Handbook of Observation & Discovery

Beaches Around the World
Botanical Drawing, Tropical Plants,
Tropical Fruits, Ocean Life,
Survival, Birds, Shells,

SARAH JANISSE BROWN

HOW TO USE THIS BOOK:

1. Take this Journal and a few pens and pencils to the beach with you.
2. Look for something inspiring, interesting, or familiar to draw or collect.
3. Some days you may want to write a poem or story about nature, animals, the weather, or your feelings.
4. You don't need to use the pages in order, use the page that you want to use each day.
5. Create a Curiosity Collection of the nonliving objects you want to draw and research at home.
6. Use a black gel pen or professional liner pen to complete the drawing lessons.

THINGS TO THINK ABOUT WHEN YOU GO OUTSIDE:

1. Think about how the beach and animals change with tides and seasons.
2. Think about how the sky and clouds look.
3. Think about how the weather feels.
4. Think about the sounds you hear near the sea.
5. Think about the animals that live near you.
6. Think about the habitats of each living creature.
7. Think about the way nature looks at different times of day.
8. Think about the way your yard changes every month.
9. Think about how to draw every detail.
10. Think about how you can do your best to appreciate, protect, and respect the environment around you.

MY NAME:

Age: Date:

By: Sarah Janisse Brown

We use the Dyslexie Font by Christian Boer
With Drawings by Susannah Brown, Brianna Faber,
Alexandra Bretush & International Illustrators

The Thinking Tree Publishing Company, LLC
FUNSCHOOLINGBOOKS.COM

Copyright 2017 ~ Do Not Copy

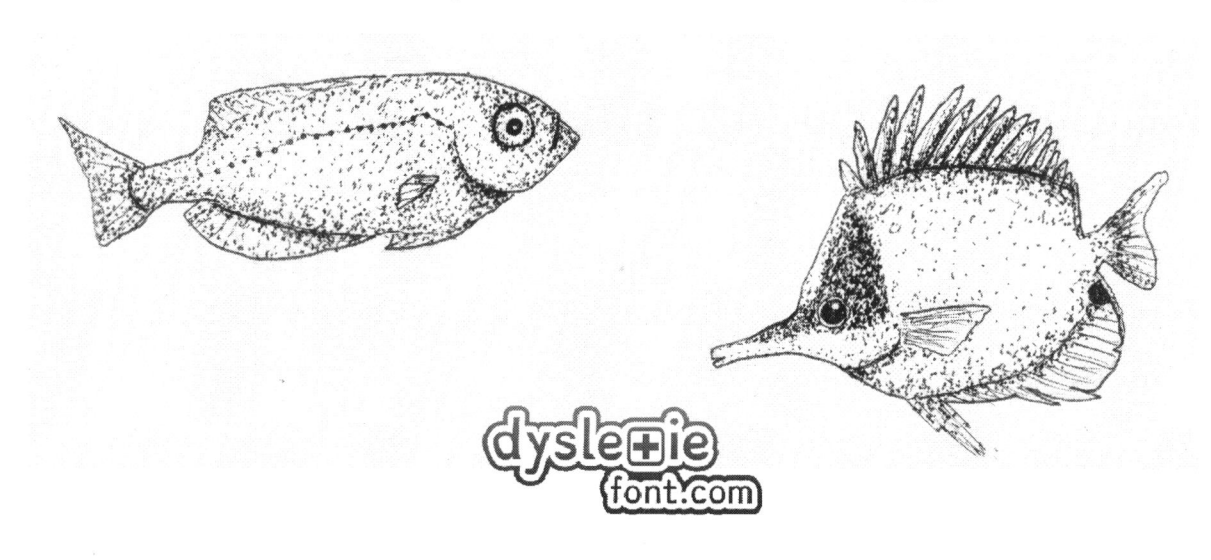

dyslexiefont.com

4

NATURE STUDY

EARTH, LAND, SKY, AND SEA
SHELL, FEATHER, CLOUD AND TREE
SAND, WATER, SUN AND SEED
PALM, FERN AND WET SEAWEED

I GENTLY GATHER LITTLE THINGS
WITHOUT DISTURBING NATURE'S SCHEMES
I LEAVE ALL LIVING THINGS ALONE
EXCEPT THE SEEDS I'LL PLANT AT HOME

I MAKE A MAP OF ALL I SAW
I LOOK, I WATCH, I PLAY AND DRAW
I FILL MY BOOK WITH MYSTERIES
OF EARTH, OF LAND. OF SKY AND SEA

SARAH JANISSE BROWN

MY BOOKS ABOUT THE SEA & NATURE:

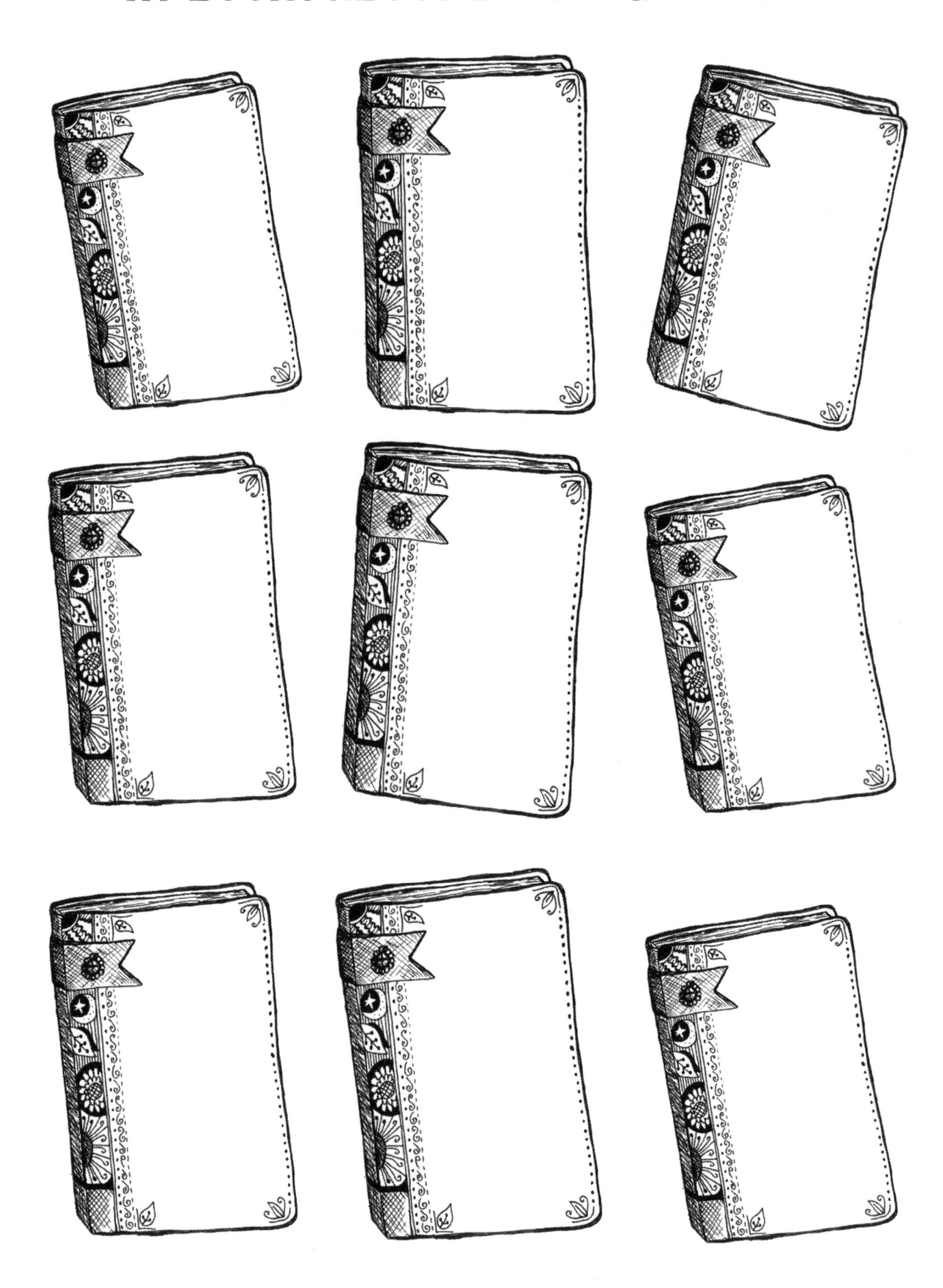

MY NATURE LIBRARY
Additional Books & Documentaries

TITLE: DATE:

My Curiosity Collection Of Drawings

This is a Collection of drawings of the things that have interested me most.

MAKE A CURIOSITY COLLECTION CABINET

Find a box, shelf or organizer you can use
to create a safe place for your nature collection.

Draw your container here:

MAKE A NATURE STUDY BASKET

Choose a basket with a strong handle and put everything you need inside for collecting objects for your cabinet. Keep tools in your basket to help you with drawing, researching, identifying and exploring nature. Be careful not to disturb living things during your adventure.

Draw your nature study basket here:

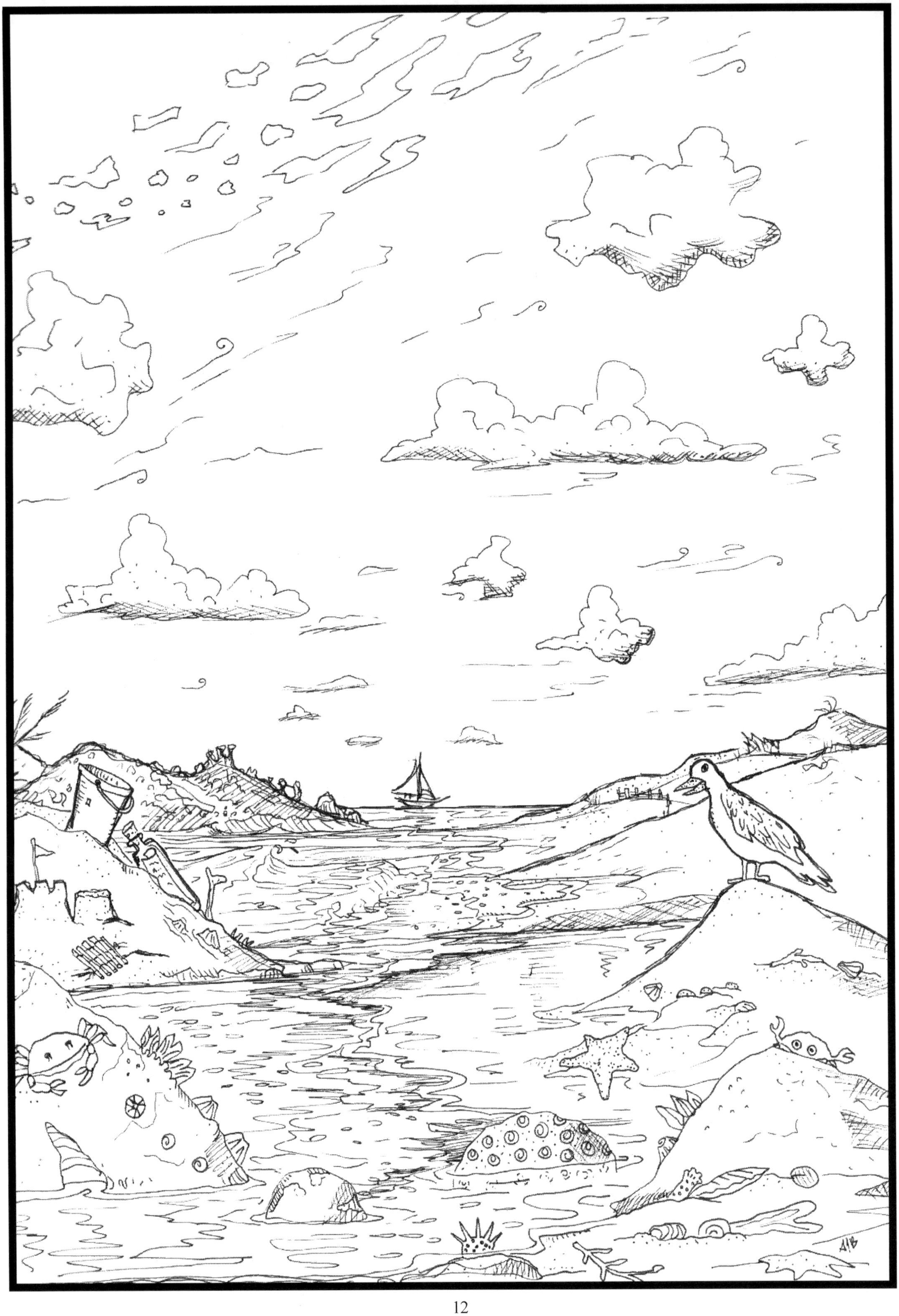

SHELL
COLLECTING
AND IDENTIFICATION

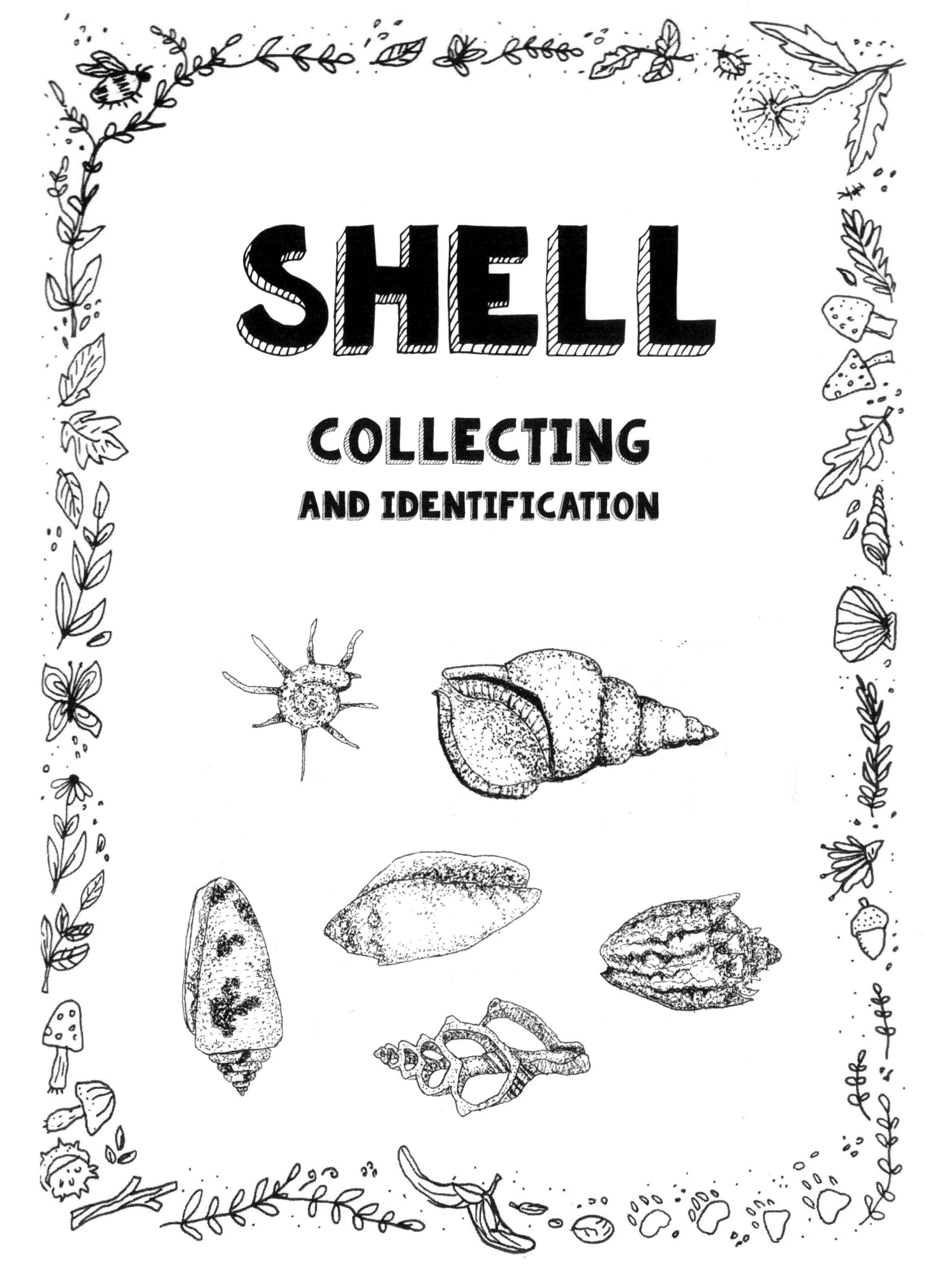

1. GIVE EACH SHELL A NEW NAME!
2. WRITE DOWN THE SCIENTIFIC NAME   3. WHERE IS THIS SHELL FOUND?

	SHARK EYE 1._____ 2._____ 3._____
	KITTEN PAW 1._____ 2._____ 3._____
	FLORIDA CONE 1._____ 2._____ 3._____
	SURF CLAM 1._____ 2._____ 3._____
	EASTERN MELAMPUS 1._____ 2._____ 3._____

Sticky notes:
- Seashells Pg. 139
- DK shells Pg 183-192
- Book of Shells Pg 31 Rice shell

1. GIVE EACH SHELL A NEW NAME!
2. WRITE DOWN THE SCIENTIFIC NAME   3. WHERE IS THIS SHELL FOUND?

	SANDY LYONSIA *(DK Shells pg 214)* 1._____ 2._____ 3._____
	BROWN BAND WENTLETRAP 1._____ 2._____ 3._____
	PURPLE DWARF OLIVE 1._____ 2._____ 3._____
	ZEBRA PERIWINKLE *(Book of Shells pg 10)* 1._____ 2._____ 3._____
	ATLANTIC PLATE LIMPET 1._____ 2._____ 3._____

1. GIVE EACH SHELL A NEW NAME!
2. WRITE DOWN THE SCIENTIFIC NAME   3. WHERE IS THIS SHELL FOUND?

BLEEDING TOOTH
1. _____
2. _____
3. _____

[sticky note: DK Shells pg 130-132]

1. _____
2. _____
3. _____

GENERAL CONE
1. _____
2. _____
3. _____

BEATIC DWARF OLIVE
1. _____
2. _____
3. _____

[sticky note: DK Shells pg 117-120] ASSA

1. _____
2. _____
3. _____

1. GIVE EACH SHELL A NEW NAME!
2. WRITE DOWN THE SCIENTIFIC NAME   3. WHERE IS THIS SHELL FOUND?

BAY SCALLOP
1. _____
2. _____
3. _____

GOULD GLASSY-BUBBLE
1. _____
2. _____
3. _____

NO[...]AIL
1. _____
2. _____
3. _____

[sticky note: Shells Book Pg 19 Cat'seye DK Shells Pg 75-77]

MARSH PERIWINKLE
1. _____
2. _____
3. _____

CHECKERED PERIWINKLE
1. _____
2. _____
3. _____

1. GIVE EACH SHELL A NEW NAME!
2. WRITE DOWN THE SCIENTIFIC NAME 3. WHERE IS THIS SHELL FOUND?

KNOBBED WHELK
1. _____
2. _____
3. _____

HEMASTOMAS
1. _____
2. _____
3. _____

Add your own shells!

1. _____
2. _____
3. _____

1. _____
2. _____
3. _____

1. _____
2. _____
3. _____

1. GIVE EACH SHELL A NEW NAME!
2. WRITE DOWN THE SCIENTIFIC NAME   3. WHERE IS THIS SHELL FOUND?

	1._____ 2._____ 3._____
	1._____ 2._____ 3._____
	1._____ 2._____ 3._____
	1._____ 2._____ 3._____
	1._____ 2._____ 3._____

1. GIVE EACH SHELL A NEW NAME!
2. WRITE DOWN THE SCIENTIFIC NAME 3. WHERE IS THIS SHELL FOUND?

Add your own shells!	1._____ 2._____ 3._____
	1._____ 2._____ 3._____
	1._____ 2._____ 3._____
	1._____ 2._____ 3._____
	1._____ 2._____ 3._____

1. GIVE EACH SHELL A NEW NAME!
2. WRITE DOWN THE SCIENTIFIC NAME   3. WHERE IS THIS SHELL FOUND?

	1._____ 2._____ 3._____
	1._____ 2._____ 3._____
	1._____ 2._____ 3._____
	1._____ 2._____ 3._____
	1._____ 2._____ 3._____

1. GIVE EACH SHELL A NEW NAME!
2. WRITE DOWN THE SCIENTIFIC NAME   3. WHERE IS THIS SHELL FOUND?

Add your own shells!	1._____ 2._____ 3._____
	1._____ 2._____ 3._____
	1._____ 2._____ 3._____
	1._____ 2._____ 3._____
	1._____ 2._____ 3._____

1. GIVE EACH SHELL A NEW NAME!
2. WRITE DOWN THE SCIENTIFIC NAME   3. WHERE IS THIS SHELL FOUND?

	1._____ 2._____ 3._____
	1._____ 2._____ 3._____
	1._____ 2._____ 3._____
	1._____ 2._____ 3._____
	1._____ 2._____ 3._____

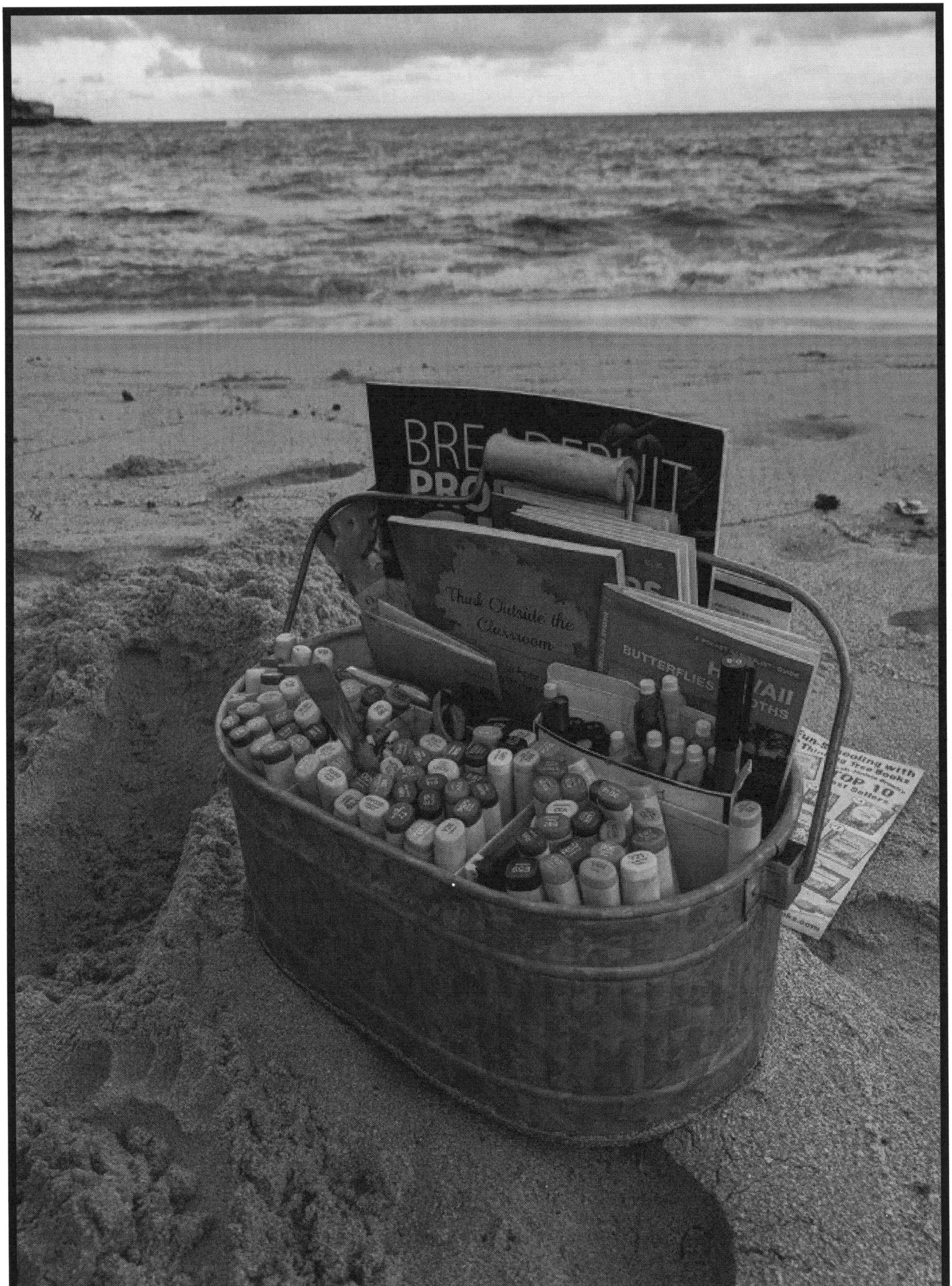
Think Outside the Classroom
BUTTERFLIES

DRAWING FROM NATURE

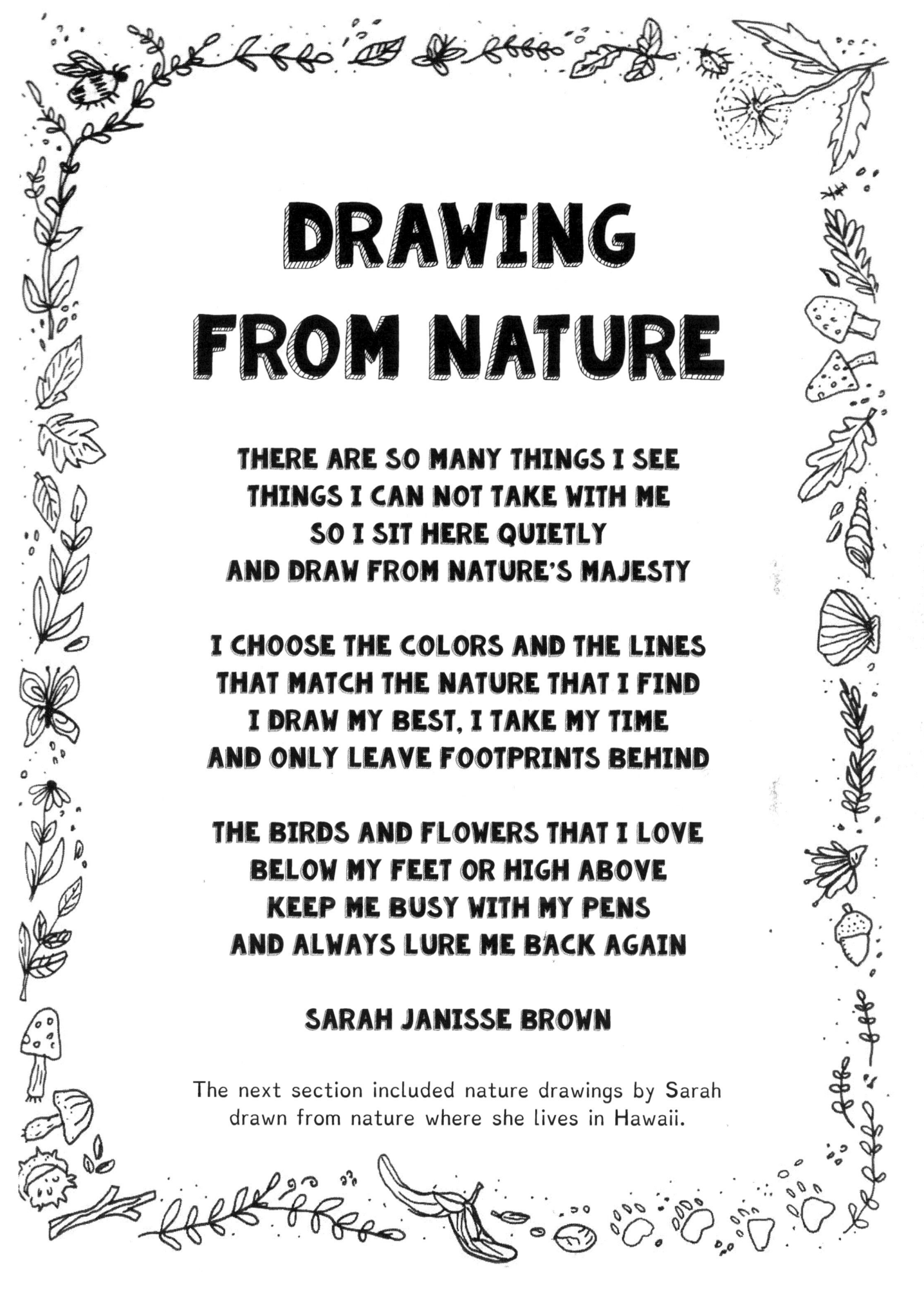

THERE ARE SO MANY THINGS I SEE
THINGS I CAN NOT TAKE WITH ME
SO I SIT HERE QUIETLY
AND DRAW FROM NATURE'S MAJESTY

I CHOOSE THE COLORS AND THE LINES
THAT MATCH THE NATURE THAT I FIND
I DRAW MY BEST, I TAKE MY TIME
AND ONLY LEAVE FOOTPRINTS BEHIND

THE BIRDS AND FLOWERS THAT I LOVE
BELOW MY FEET OR HIGH ABOVE
KEEP ME BUSY WITH MY PENS
AND ALWAYS LURE ME BACK AGAIN

SARAH JANISSE BROWN

The next section included nature drawings by Sarah drawn from nature where she lives in Hawaii.

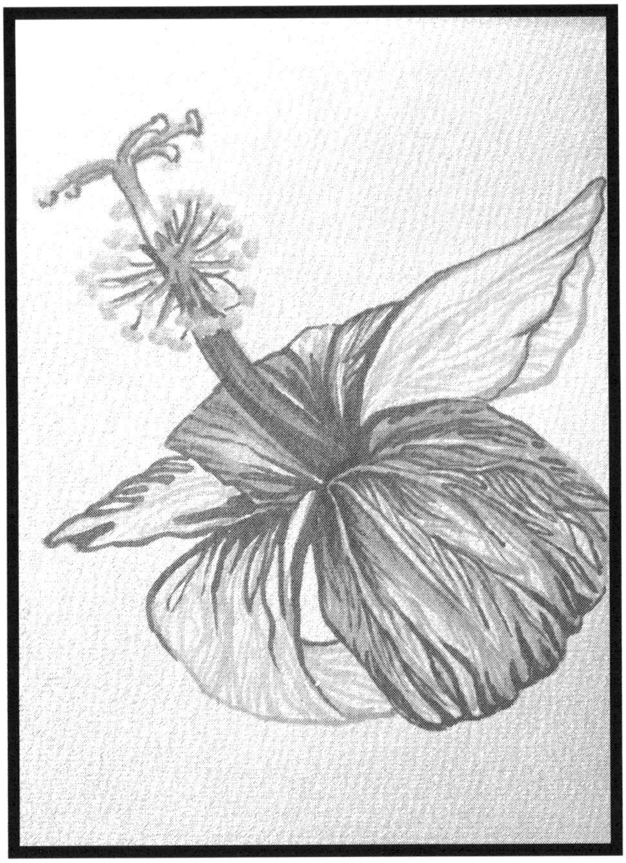

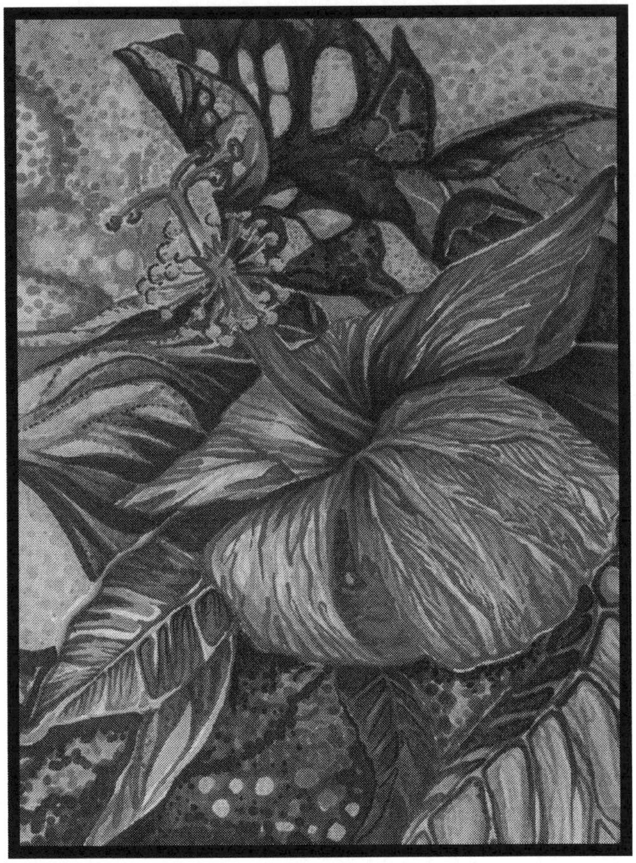

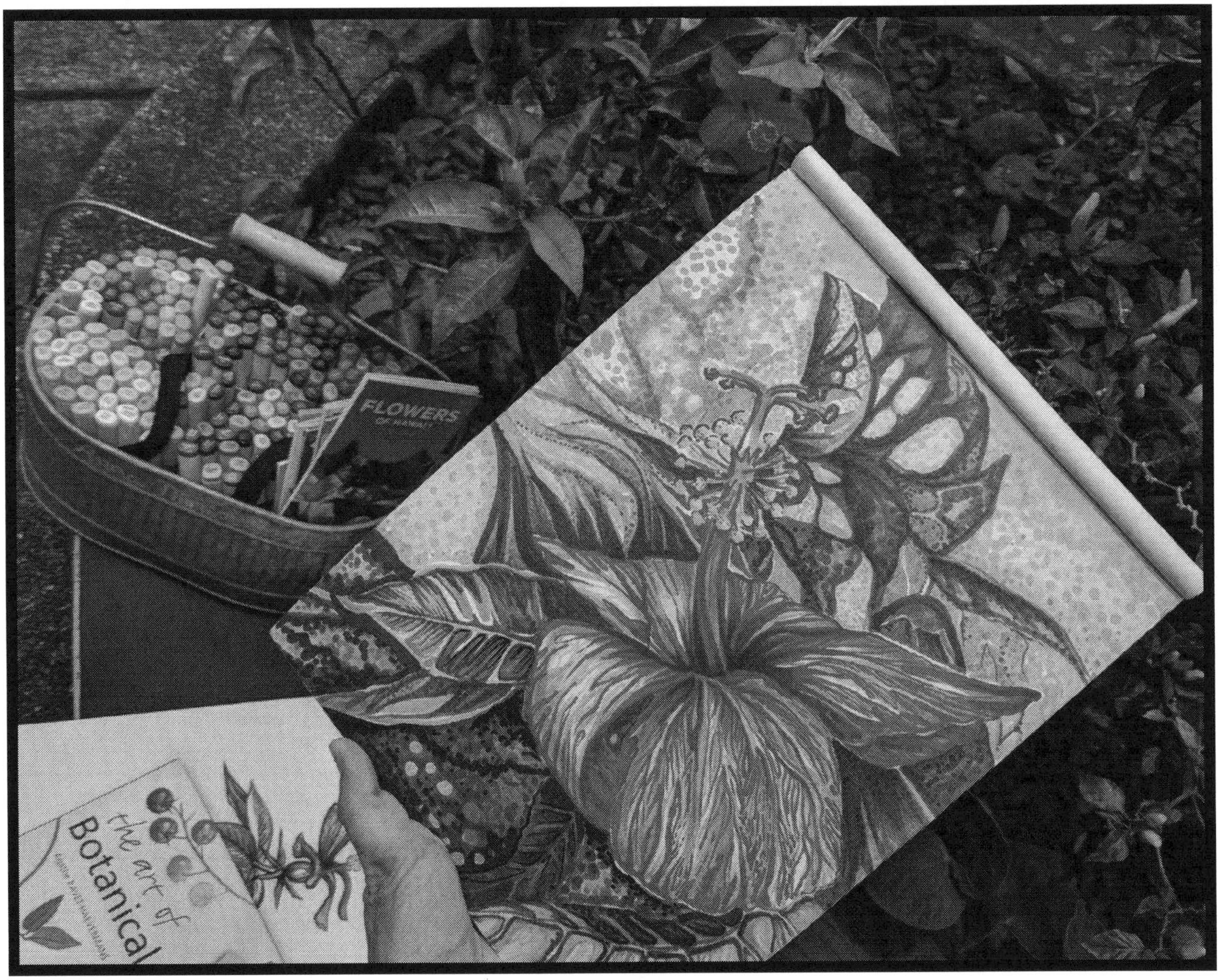
FLOWERS
the art of
Botanical

BY SARAH JANISSE BROWN

Sarah drew this rare Clayi Hibiscus Flower in August 2018.
It was growing in her garden.
She used Copic Markers.
Try drawing from nature too!

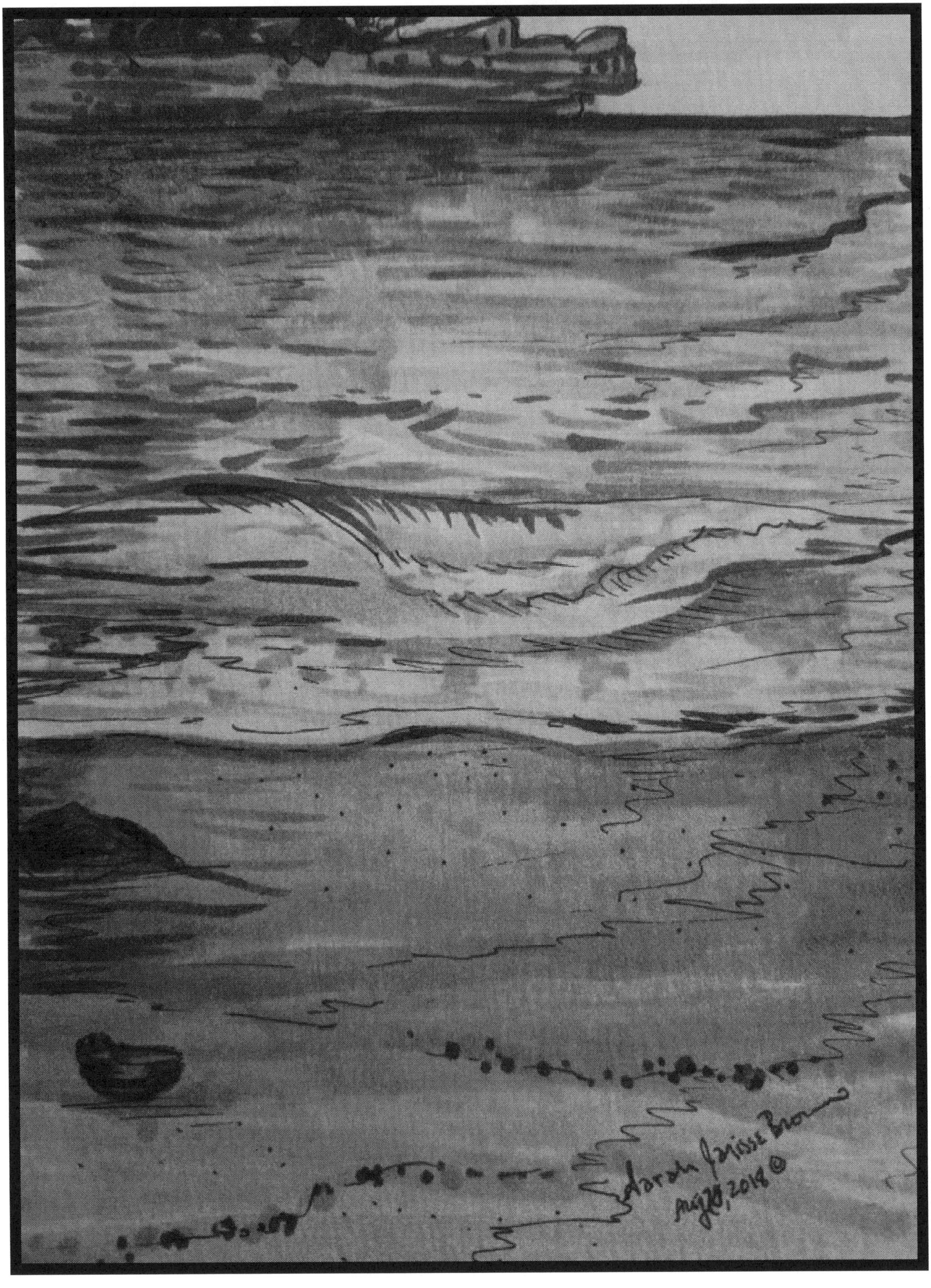

MAHA'ULEPU HERITAGE TRAIL
BY SARAH JANISSE BROWN
WRITE DOWN FOUR FACTS ABOUT THIS UNIQUE PLACE IN KAUAI, HAWAII

1. _____
2. _____
3. _____
4. _____

SARAH LOVES TO DRAW FROM NATURE, SHE BRINGS HER ART SUPPLIES WITH HER ON FIELD TRIPS SO SHE CAN DRAW NATURE.

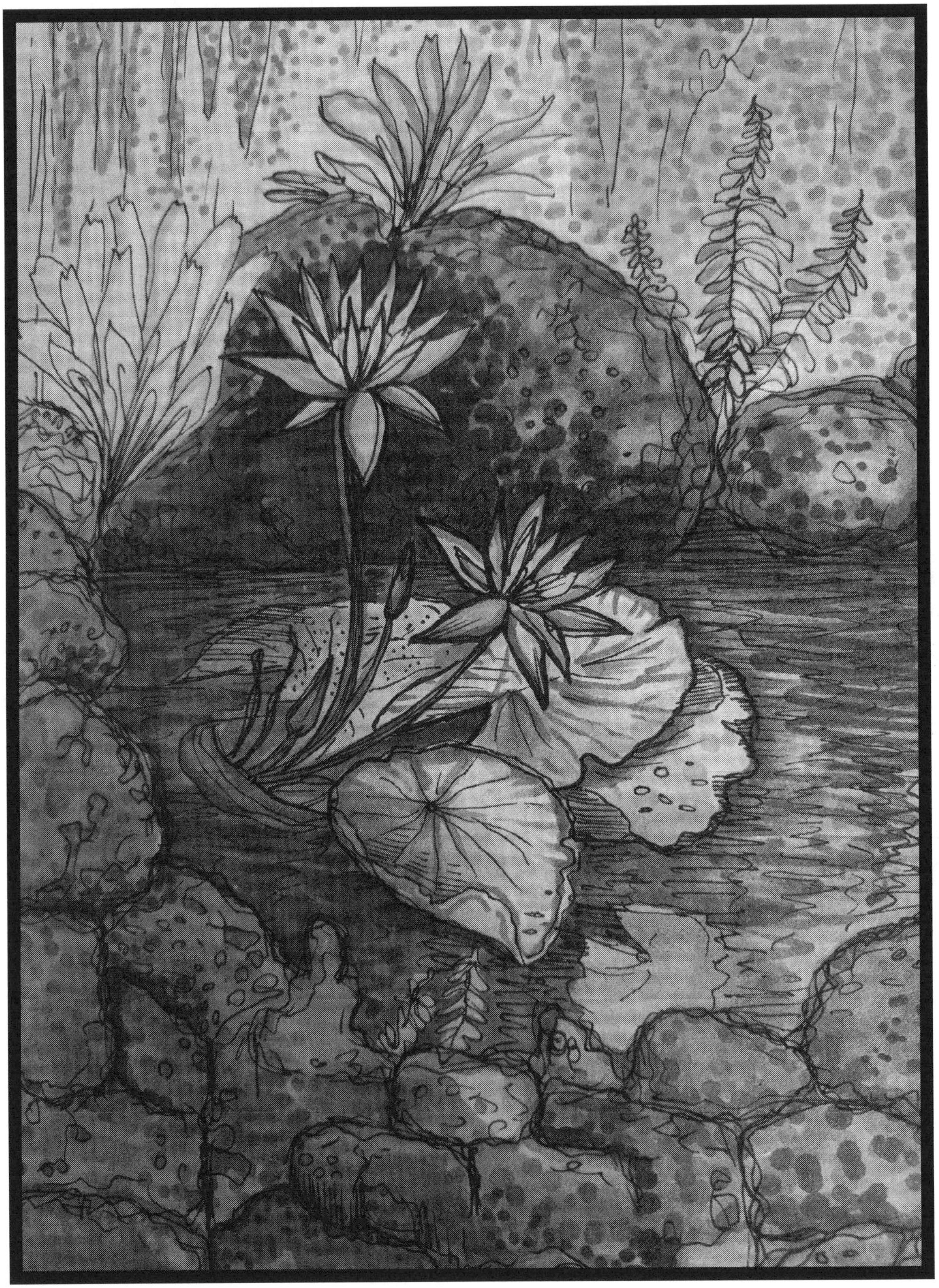

WATER LILIES
BY SARAH JANISSE BROWN
WRITE DOWN FOUR FACTS ABOUT THIS PLANT

1. _____
2. _____
3. _____
4. _____

DRAW A FLOWER FROM YOUR NEIGHBORHOOD!

Sarah drew this picture when she was on a field trip with her children at the National Botanical Tropic Gardens near her home in Kauai, Hawaii.

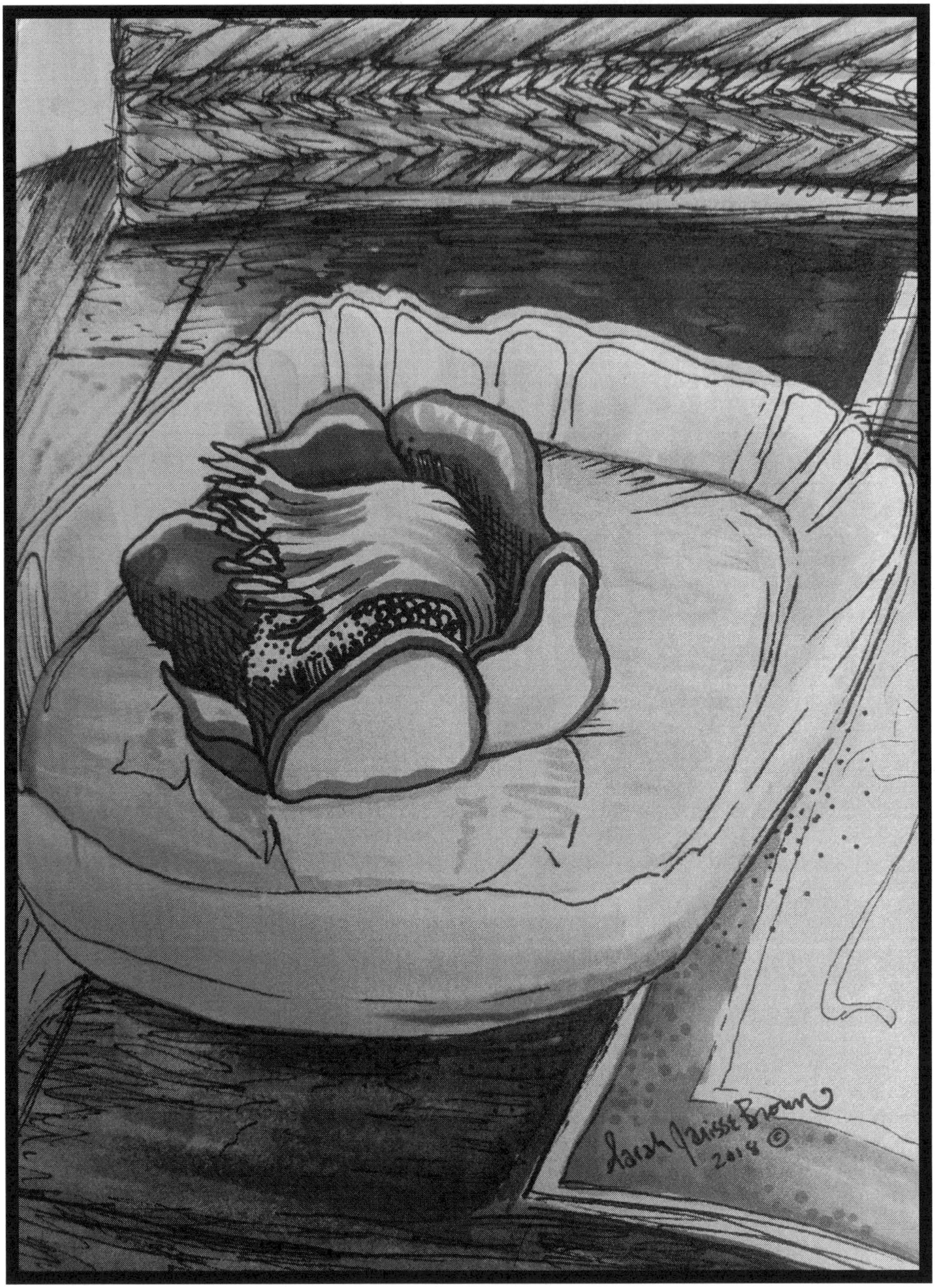
Brown
2018 ©

CANNONBALL FLOWER
BY SARAH JANISSE BROWN
WRITE DOWN FOUR FACTS ABOUT THIS PLANT

1. _____
2. _____
3. _____
4. _____

DRAW A FLOWER THAT YOU HAVE PICKED.

Sarah drew this picture at home after a tour guide gave her this flower at National Botanical Tropic Gardens.

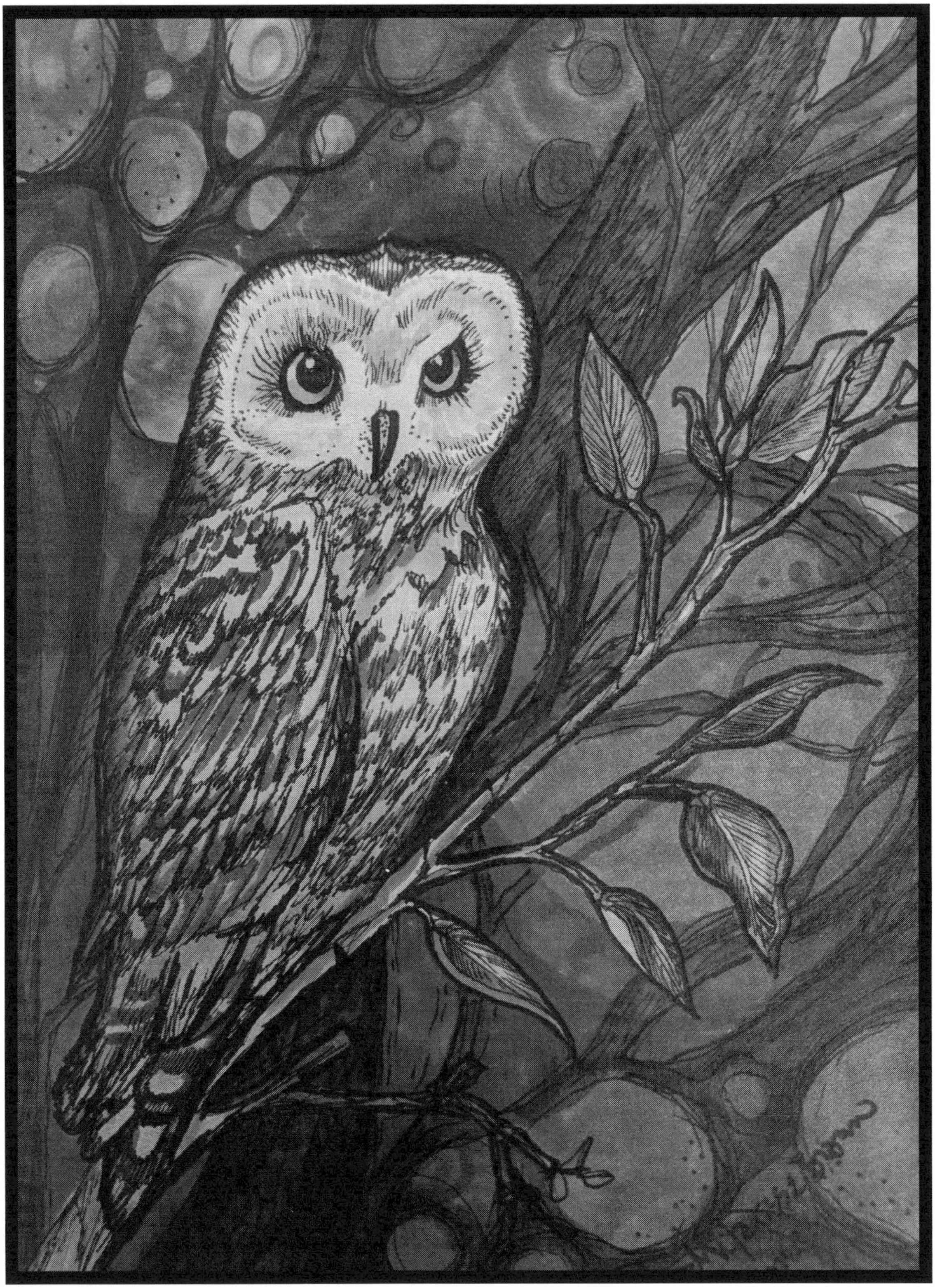

PUEO HAWAIIAN OWL
BY SARAH JANISSE BROWN
WRITE DOWN FOUR FACTS ABOUT THIS BIRD

1. _____
2. _____
3. _____
4. _____

DRAW AN OWL THAT LIVES IN YOUR AREA

Sarah drew this picture from a book when she wanted to learn more about endangered birds that live in her area.

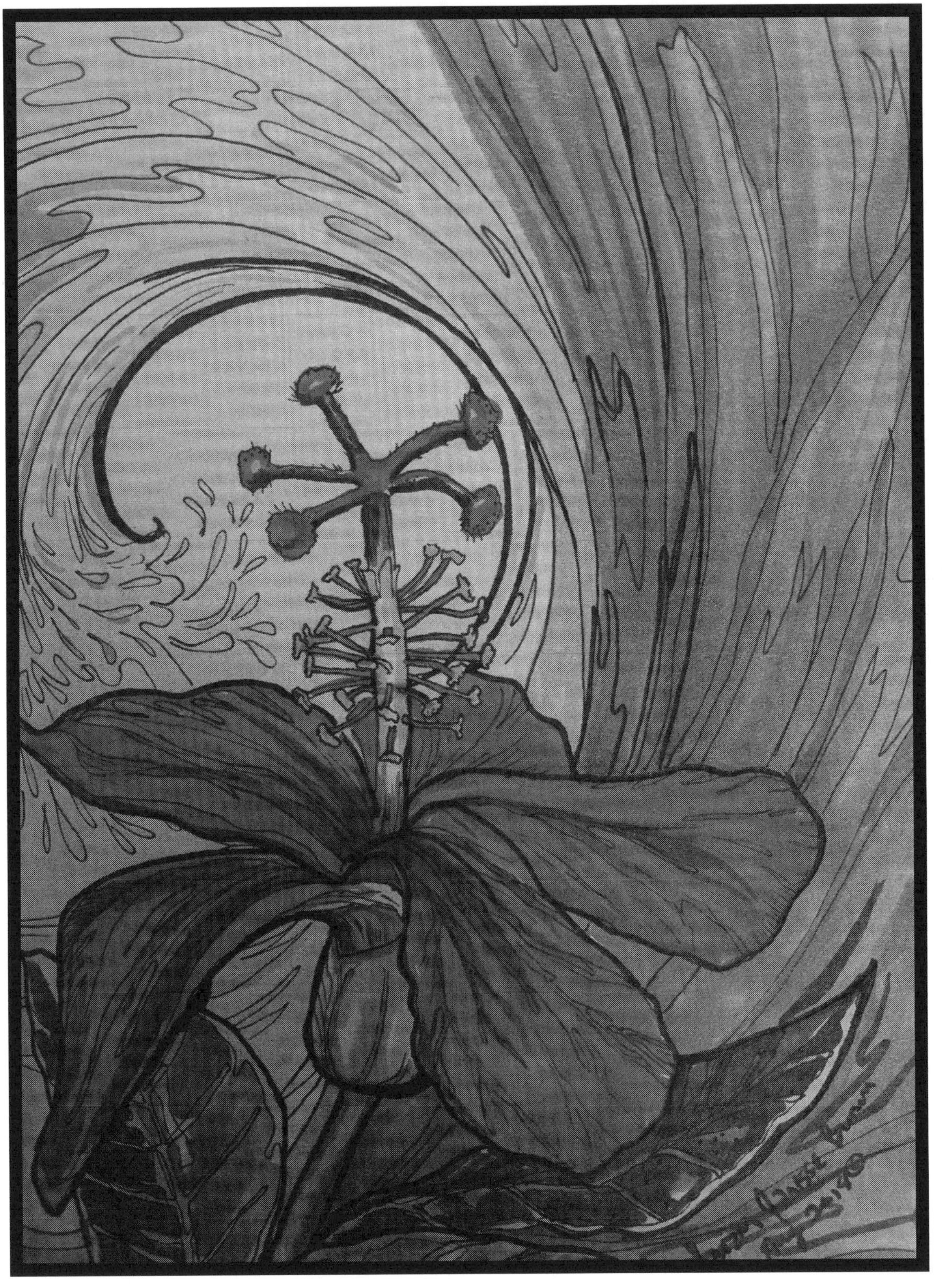

CLAYI HIBISCUS
BY SARAH JANISSE BROWN
WRITE DOWN FOUR FACTS ABOUT THIS ENDANGERED PLANT

1. _____
2. _____
3. _____
4. _____

DRAW A RARE PLANT THE GROWS IN YOUR AREA.

Sarah loves rare plants and animals. There are less than 80 Clayi Hibiscus plants in the world, there are only four lft in the wild. Two of these plants are growing in Sarah's Garden. Many are growing at the National Topical Botanical Garden in Kauai.

By planting rare plants, native plants, and heirloom plants we can keep species from going extinct.

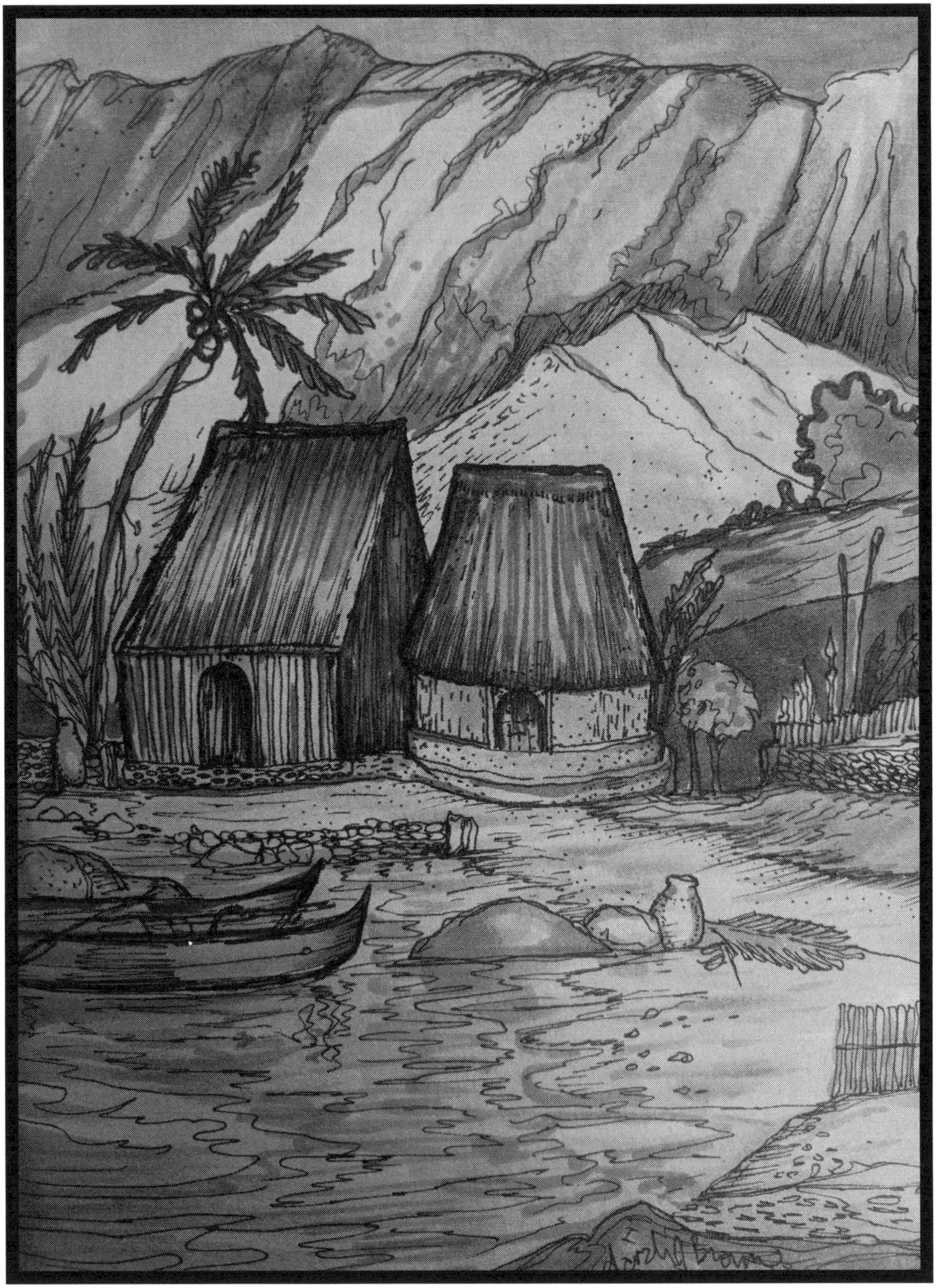

POLYNESIAN CANOE PEOPLE
BY SARAH JANISSE BROWN
WRITE DOWN FOUR FACTS ABOUT THESE PACIFIC VOYAGERS

1. _____
2. _____
3. _____
4. _____

DRAW THE HOMES OF THE NATIVE PEOPLE WHO ONCE LIVED IN YOUR AREA.

Sarah was curious about the people who first settled her island. She looked in many books to learn about the native people of Hawaii. This is how their homes and canoes may have looked.

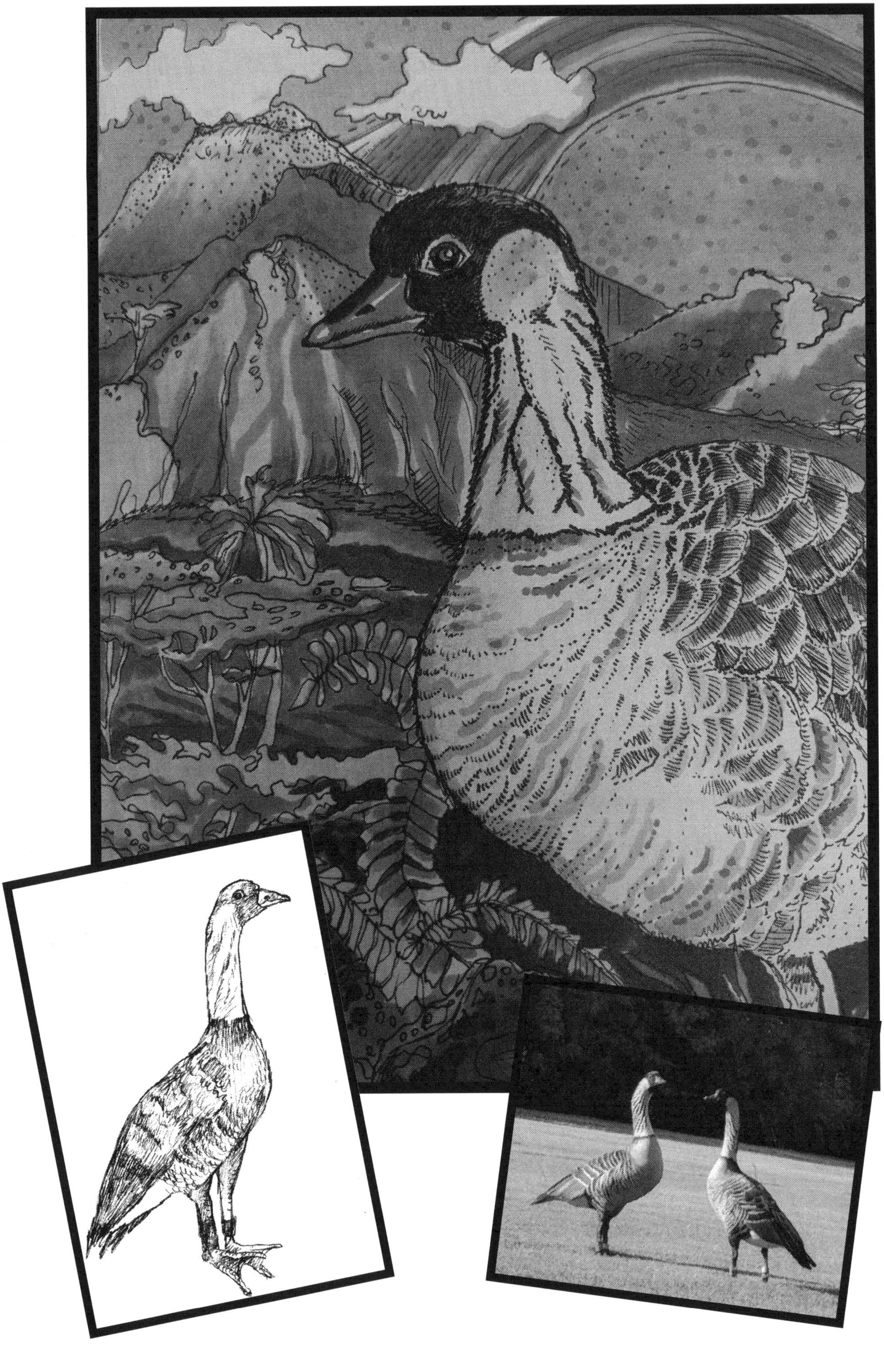

HAWAIIAN NE NE GOOSE

BY SARAH JANISSE BROWN
WRITE DOWN FOUR FACTS ABOUT THIS ENDANGERED BIRD

1. _____
2. _____
3. _____
4. _____

DRAW YOUR STATE BIRD OR TAKE A PHOTO OF ONE!

Sarah drew this picture from a book when she wanted to learn more about the state bird of Hawaii. She also took a picture of a pair of Ne Ne Geese she saw on a Field Trip.

A PHOTOGRAPHIC GUIDE TO THE
BIRDS OF HAWAI'I
THE MAIN ISLANDS AND OFFSHORE WATERS
The Thinking Tree
WILD WILDERNESS
ADVENTURE HANDBOOK
A SURVIVAL GUIDE
A SCIENCE JOURNAL
Botanical Drawing
A STEP-BY-STEP GUIDE TO DRAWING FLOWERS, VEGETABLES, FRUIT AND OTHER PLANT LIFE
PENNY BROWN
The Thinking Tree
NATURE STUDY
& OUTDOOR SCIENCE
JOURNAL
art of
otanical Drawing
AN INTRODUCTORY GUIDE
SMITHSONIAN
DK
ROCK & FOSSIL
HUNTER
EXPERIMENTS & ACTIVITI
Star Advertiser
Timeline
Hawai'i
ANCIENT SITES OF KAUA'I
A Guide to Hawaiian Archaeological and Cultural Places
A PARENTS' CHOICE APPROVED AWARD WINNER
Nature's
From t-shirts to twig baskets, 65 cool projects for crafty kids
Art
make with natural materials you can find anywhere
Written by Laura C. Martin with drawings by David Cain
In the Beginning
ARCHIPELAGO
THE ORIGIN AND DISCOVERY OF THE HAWAIIAN ISLANDS
Plants of the Canoe People
W. Arthur Whistler

MY NATURE LIBRARY

IT'S RAINING OUTSIDE
THE WIND BLOWS HARD
I CAN NOT GO EXPLORE MY YARD
I'LL STAY INSIDE
AND TAKE A LOOK
AT ALL THE NATURE IN MY BOOKS

I'LL READ THE STORIES
OF THE SEAS
I'LL LOOK AT PICTURES OF THE TREES
I'LL SEARCH FOR BIRDS,
AND SHELLS AND LEAVES
TURNING PAGES AS I PLEASE

I'LL RESEARCH THE CREATURES
I HAVE FOUND
IN THE SKY
AND ON THE GROUND
I'LL LEARN ABOUT THE BEACH AND SEA
THOUGH MY OWN NATURE LIBRARY

SARAH JANISSE BROWN

Choose a book from your nature library to read today. Document your learning with words and pictures here!

READING TIME

Today's Date: _____

DRAW A PICTURE FROM ONE OF YOUR NATURE BOOKS ABOUT ANIMALS

LIST THE FLYING ANIMALS THAT LIVE IN YOUR AREA:

_____
_____
_____
_____
_____
_____
_____
_____
_____
_____
_____
_____
_____
_____

LIST THE FLYING ANIMALS THAT LIVE IN YOUR AREA:

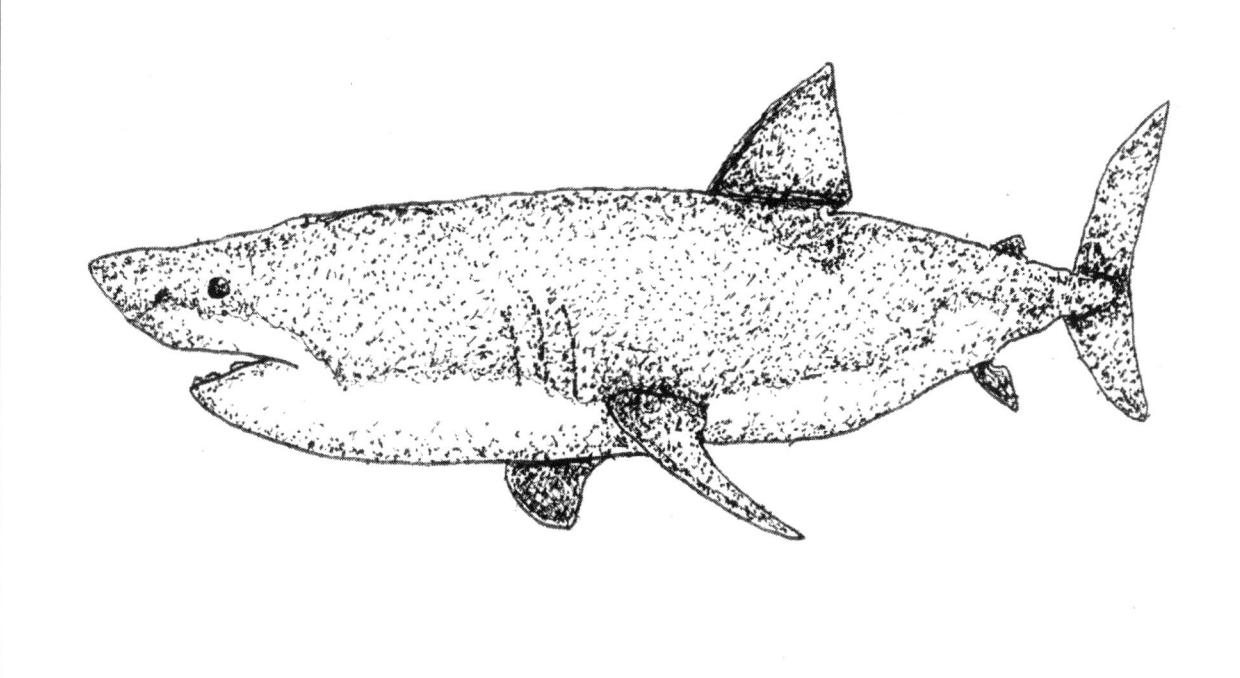

LIST THE DANGEROUS ANIMALS THAT LIVE IN YOUR AREA:

_____
_____
_____
_____
_____
_____
_____
_____
_____
_____
_____
_____
_____
_____

LIST THE DANGEROUS ANIMALS THAT LIVE IN YOUR AREA:

**DRAW A PICTURE OF
YOUR FAVORITE OCEAN ANIMAL**

RESEARCH YOUR FAVORITE FISH

Choose a book from your nature library to read today. Document your learning with words and pictures here!

READING TIME

Today's Date:

DRAW A PICTURE FROM ONE OF YOUR NATURE BOOKS ABOUT PLANTS

COMMON NAME:

Orchid

What is the Scientific Name:

_____

RESEARCH THIS PLANT

What can this plant be used for?

_____   _____
_____   _____
_____   _____

Where did it originate?
_____
_____

Where else can it be found?
_____
_____

How did it travel to other parts of the world?
_____
_____

Is this plant in danger of extinction? Why or Why Not?
_____
_____

ANIMALS IN MY REGION

What animal are you learning about?

Common Name:_____

Scientific Name:_____

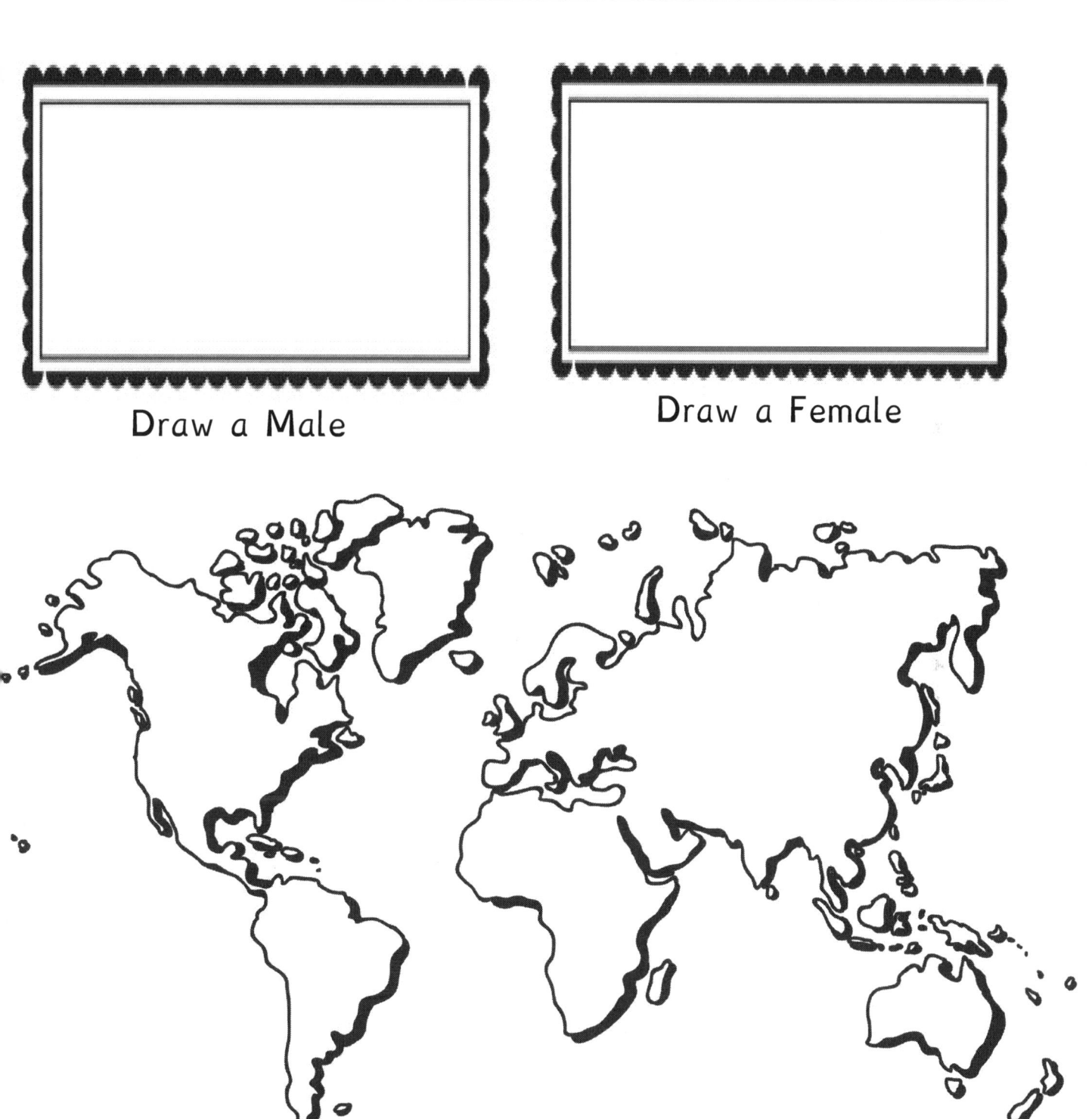

Draw a Male

Draw a Female

Color the other parts of the world where this animal lives.

COLOR AND RESEARCH
EACH OF THESE REALISTIC DRAWINGS

1. Strelitzia   2. Passiflora   3. Heliconia   4. Nerium Oleander   5. King Protea

DRAW TWO OF YOUR FAVORITES WITH A FINE POINT BLACK PEN.

6. Prosthechea   7. Hibiscus   8. Orange Blossom   9. Camellia   10. Magnolia

USE A CAMERA TO TAKE PICTURES OF NATURE

Print your photos and place them here:

Choose a book from your nature library to read today. Document your learning with words and pictures here!

Today's Date: _____

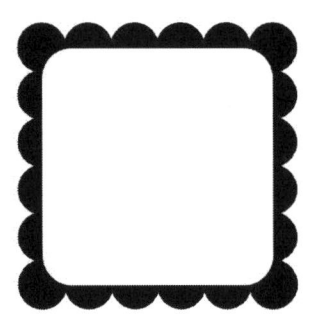

READING TIME

**DRAW A PICTURE FROM ONE OF YOUR
NATURE BOOKS ABOUT BEACHES**

STUDY AND COMPARE THESE TWO BEACHES

Beach #1 The Island of Capri, Italy

Beach #2 Black Sand Beach, Alaska, USA

Contact the local wildlife society or nature center to learn more!

DRAW 2 SHELLS THAT CAN BE FOUND ON EACH BEACH.

Beach #1   Beach #2

LIST 4 LAND ANIMALS THAT CAN BE FOUND AT EACH BEACH

_____   _____
_____   _____
_____   _____
_____   _____

LIST 4 SEA CREATURES THAT CAN BE FOUND NEAR THIS BEACH

_____   _____
_____   _____
_____   _____
_____   _____

LIST 4 BIRDS THAT CAN BE SPOTTED NEAR THIS BEACH

_____   _____
_____   _____
_____   _____
_____   _____

STUDY THE CLOUDS AND THE WEATHER

DRAW THE CLOUDS AND THE WEATHER

WATCH A DOCUMENTARY OR READ A BOOK ABOUT THE ANIMALS THAT LIVE IN OCEANS AND TIDE POOLS.

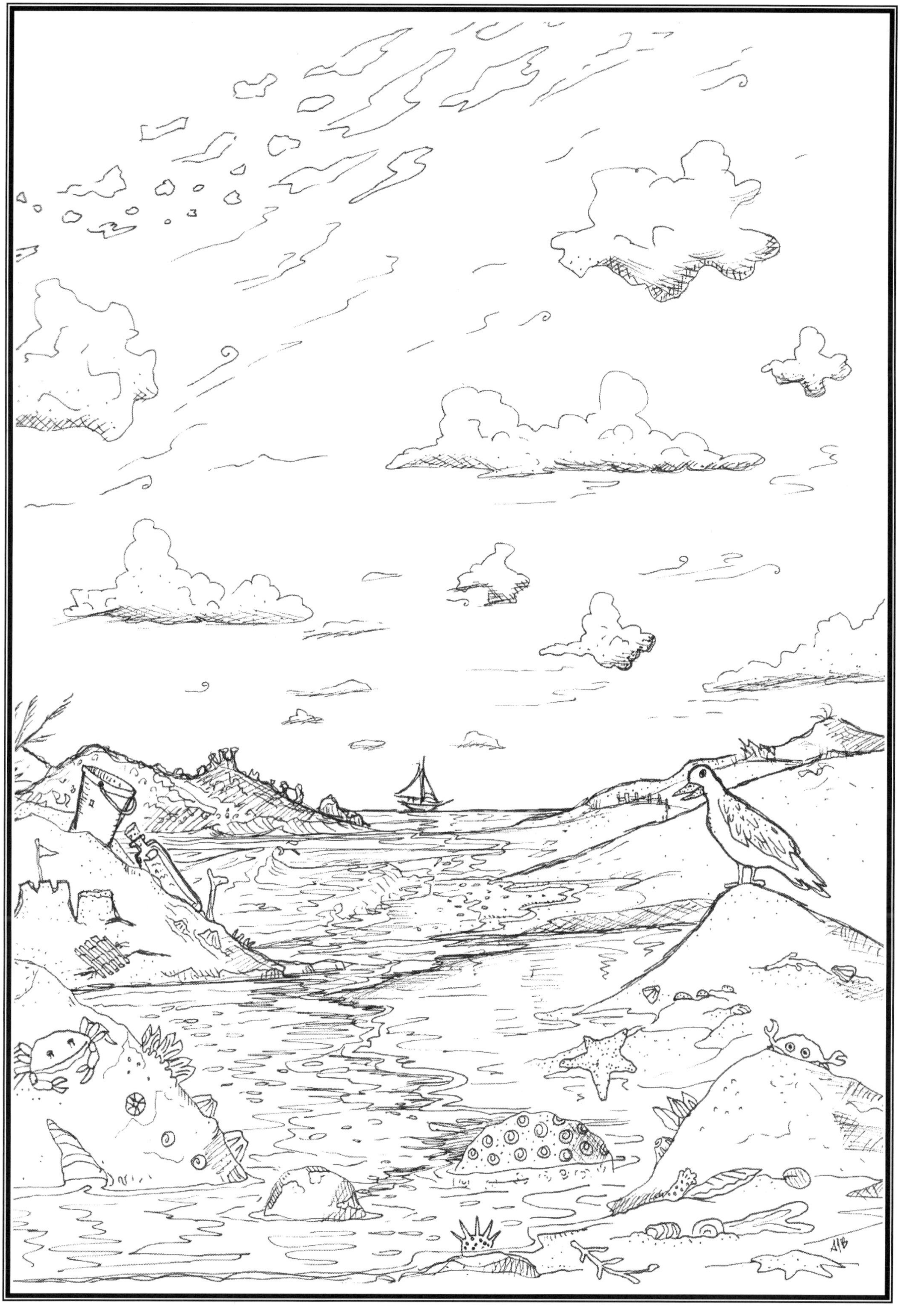

COMMON NAME:

Hibiscus

What is the Scientific Name:

_____

RESEARCH THIS PLANT

What can this plant be used for?

_____
_____   _____
_____   _____

Where did it originate?

_____
_____

Where else can it be found?

_____
_____

How did it travel to other parts of the world?

_____
_____

Is this plant in danger of extinction? Why or Why Not?

_____
_____

ANIMALS IN MY REGION

What animal are you learning about?

Common Name:_____

Scientific Name:_____

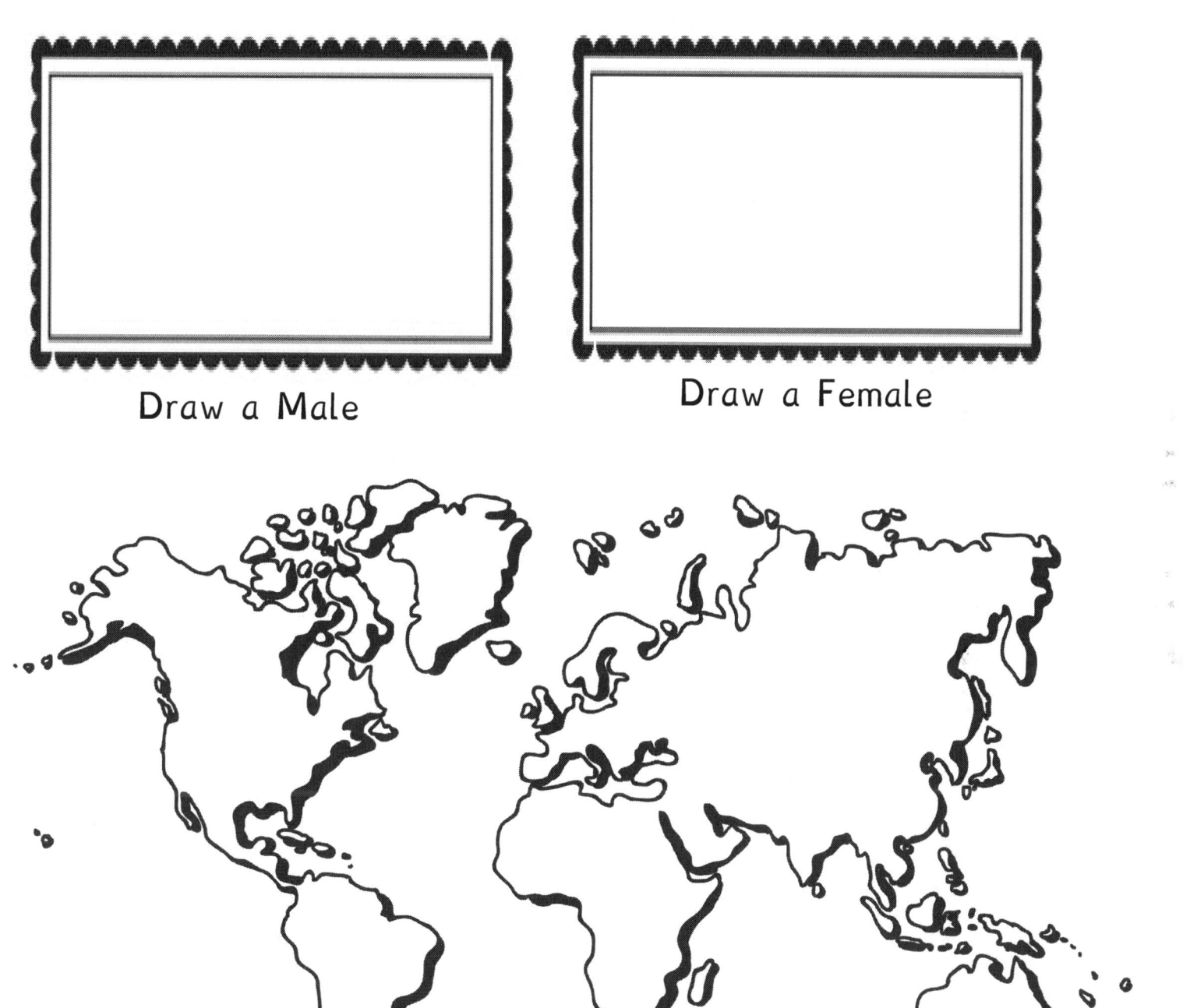

Draw a Male

Draw a Female

Color the other parts of the world where this animal lives.

67

COLOR AND RESEARCH
EACH OF THESE REALISTIC DRAWINGS

1. Magnolia   2. Begonia   3. Vriesea   4. Gardenia   5. Plumeria   6. Cymbidium

68

DRAW TWO OF YOUR FAVORITES WITH A FINE POINT BLACK PEN.

7. Phalaenopsis Schilleriana   8. Curcuma   9. Calla   10. Amaryllis   11. Tuberosa

STUDY AND COMPARE THESE TWO BEACHES

Beach #1   Montego Bay, Jamaica

Beach #2   Holly Beach in Cameron Parish Louisiana, USA

Contact the local wildlife society or nature center to learn more!

DRAW 2 SHELLS THAT CAN BE FOUND ON EACH BEACH.

Beach #1   Beach #2

LIST 4 LAND ANIMALS THAT CAN BE FOUND AT EACH BEACH

_____   _____
_____   _____
_____   _____
_____   _____

LIST 4 SEA CREATURES THAT CAN BE FOUND NEAR THIS BEACH

_____   _____
_____   _____
_____   _____
_____   _____

LIST 4 BIRDS THAT CAN BE SPOTTED NEAR THIS BEACH

_____   _____
_____   _____
_____   _____
_____   _____

Choose a book from your nature library to read today. Document your learning with words and pictures here!

Today's Date:

READING TIME

COLLECT 10 SMALL THINGS FROM YOUR YARD AND MAKE A NATURE CRAFT.

1. COLOR

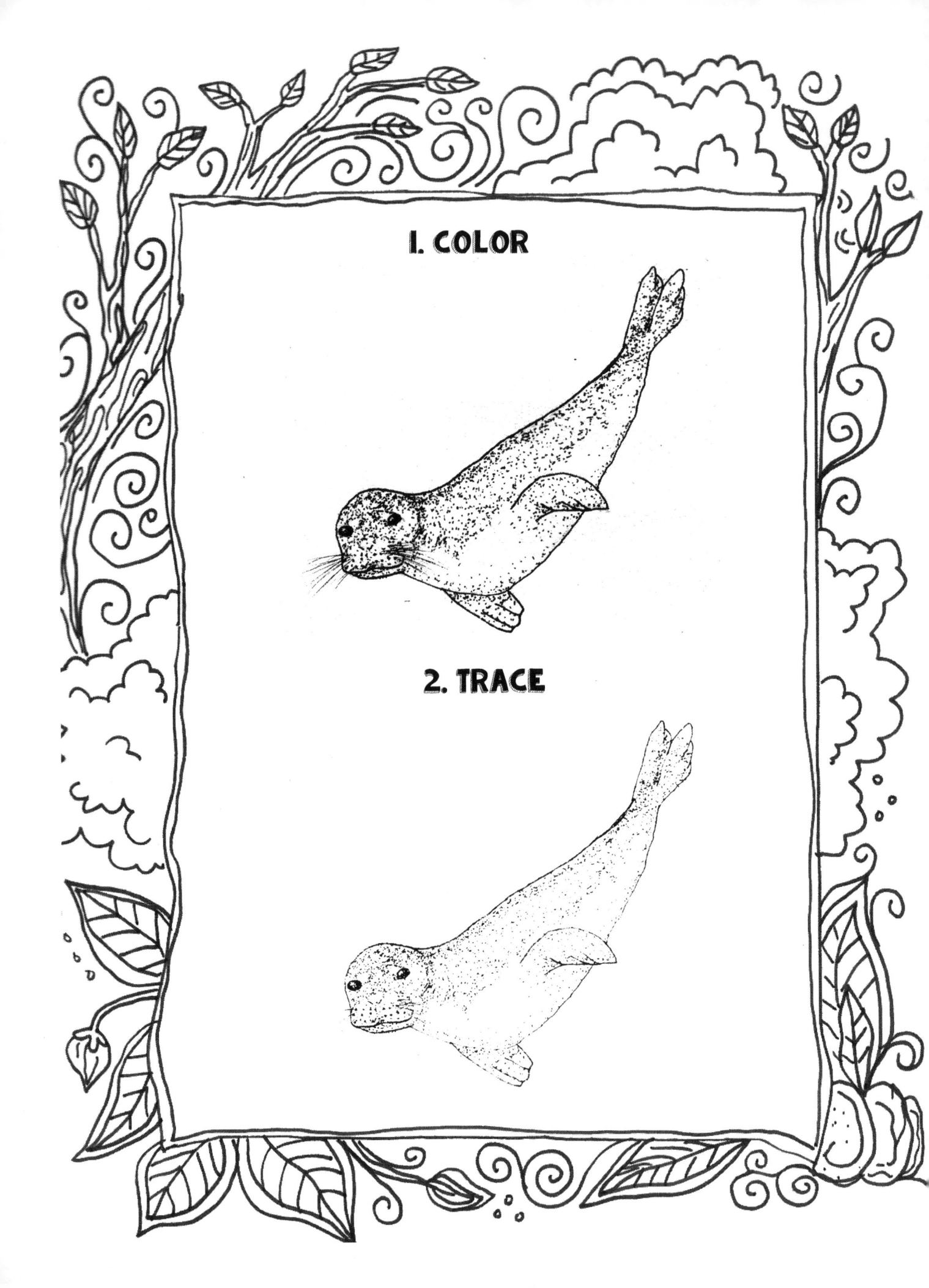

2. TRACE

3. DRAW THE MISSING PART:

4. DRAW THE ANIMAL:

COMMON NAME:

Bird of Paradise

What is the Scientific Name:

_____

RESEARCH THIS PLANT

What can this plant be used for?

_____   _____
_____   _____
_____   _____

Where did it originate?

_____
_____

Where else can it be found?

_____
_____

How did it travel to other parts of the world?

_____
_____

Is this plant in danger of extinction? Why or Why Not?

_____
_____

ANIMALS IN MY REGION

What animal are you learning about?

Common Name:_____

Scientific Name:_____

Draw a Male

Draw a Female

Color the other parts of the world where this animal lives.

COLOR AND RESEARCH
EACH OF THESE REALISTIC DRAWINGS

1
2
3
6
7
8

1. Banana Palm.   2. Cordyline.   3. Areca Palm.   4. Alocasia.   5. Fern.   6. Tahiti   7. Monstera

DRAW TWO OF YOUR FAVORITES WITH A FINE POINT BLACK PEN.

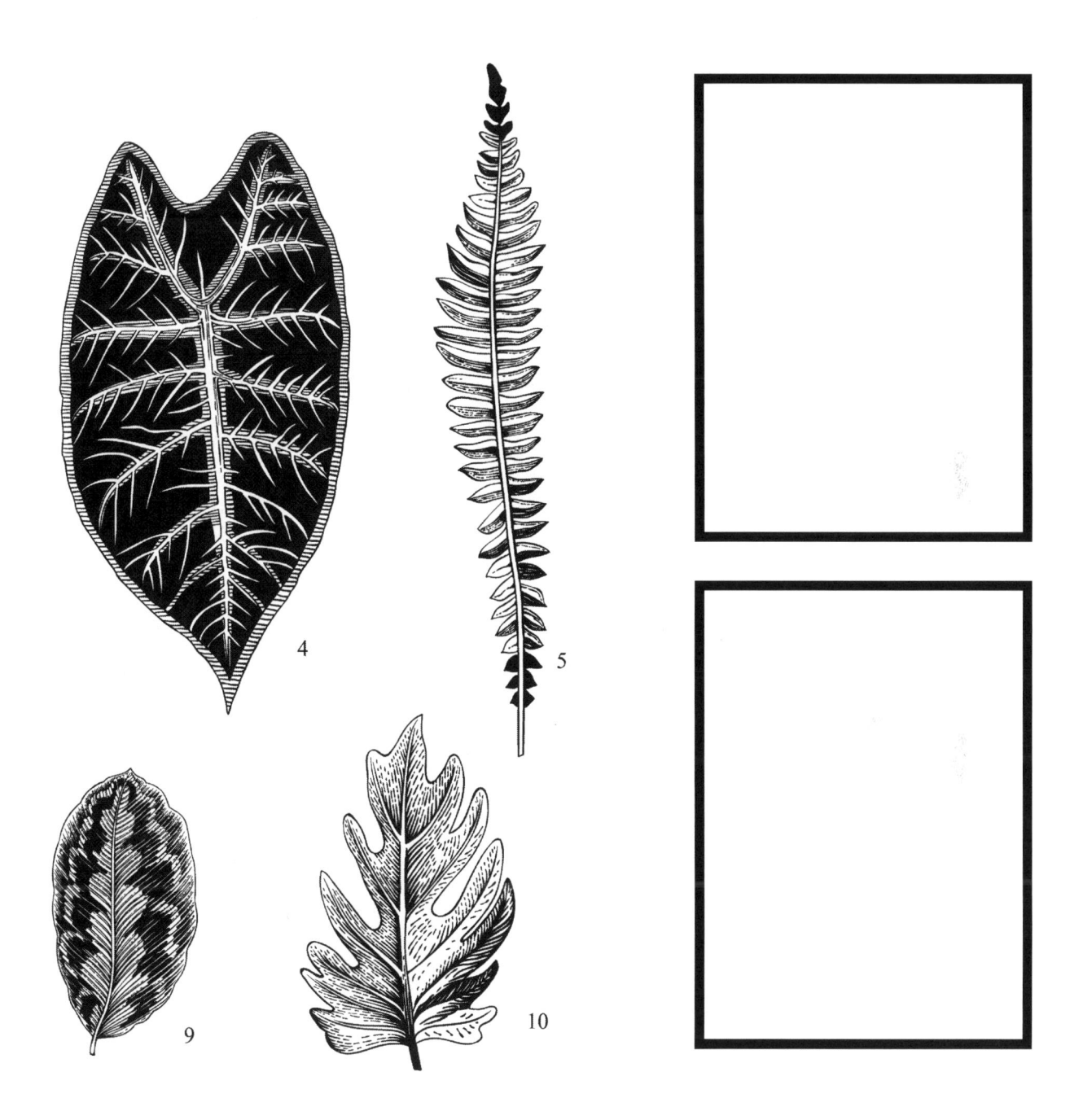

8. Codiaeum.   9. Calathea.   10. Philodendron.

STUDY AND COMPARE THESE TWO BEACHES

Beach #1 Cola beach, South GOA, India.

Beach #2 Chrystal Beach, Texas, USA

Contact the local wildlife society or nature center to learn more!

DRAW 2 SHELLS THAT CAN BE FOUND ON EACH BEACH.

Beach #1   Beach #2

LIST 4 LAND ANIMALS THAT CAN BE FOUND AT EACH BEACH

LIST 4 SEA CREATURES THAT CAN BE FOUND NEAR THIS BEACH

LIST 4 BIRDS THAT CAN BE SPOTTED NEAR THIS BEACH

COLLECT 10 SMALL THINGS FROM NATURE AND MAKE A NATURE CRAFT.

DRAW SMALL THINGS YOU SEE OUTSIDE

FIND AND COLOR IN THE HIDDEN OBJECTS

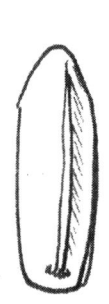

GO OUTSIDE AND DRAW AN INSECT IN EACH BOX

Choose a book from your nature library to read today. Document your learning with words and pictures here!

READING TIME

Today's Date: _____

DRAW A PICTURE FROM ONE OF YOUR NATURE BOOKS ABOUT AN ENDANGERED ANIMALS

COMMON NAME:

Heliconia

What is the Scientific Name:

_____

RESEARCH THIS PLANT

What can this plant be used for?

_____ _____
_____ _____
_____ _____

Where did it originate?

_____
_____

Where else can it be found?

_____
_____

How did it travel to other parts of the world?

_____
_____

Is this plant in danger of extinction? Why or Why Not?

_____
_____

ANIMALS IN MY REGION

What animal are you learning about?
Common Name:_____
Scientific Name:_____

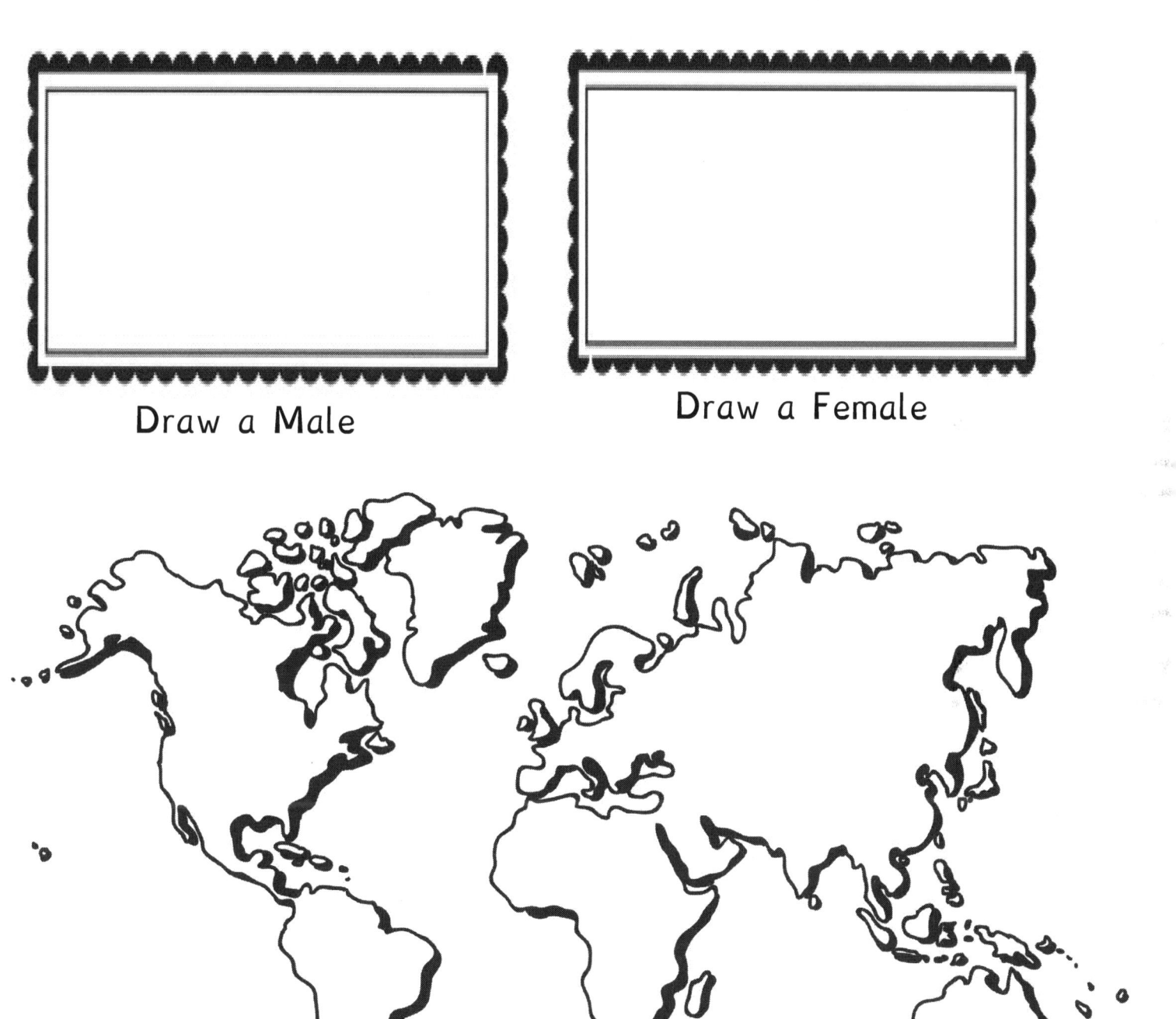

Draw a Male

Draw a Female

Color the other parts of the world where this animal lives.

89

COLOR AND RESEARCH EACH OF THESE REALISTIC DRAWINGS

1. Mallow. 2. Poppy. 3. Anemone. 4. Tulip. 5. Delphinium. 6. Chrysanthemum. 7. Rose. 8. Primula

DRAW TWO OF YOUR FAVORITES WITH A FINE POINT BLACK PEN.

9. Sweet-William. 10. Fritillaria. 11. Aster. 12. Hydrangea. 13. **Forget-Me-Not** 14. Petunia

STUDY AND COMPARE THESE TWO BEACHES

Beach #1 Canopied beach at the Baltic Coast, Island Rugia, Germany

Beach #2 Bethany Beach, Delaware, USA

Contact the local wildlife society or nature center to learn more!

DRAW 2 SHELLS THAT CAN BE FOUND ON EACH BEACH.

Beach #1   Beach #2

LIST 4 LAND ANIMALS THAT CAN BE FOUND AT EACH BEACH

_____   _____
_____   _____
_____   _____
_____   _____

LIST 4 SEA CREATURES THAT CAN BE FOUND NEAR THIS BEACH

_____   _____
_____   _____
_____   _____
_____   _____

LIST 4 BIRDS THAT CAN BE SPOTTED NEAR THIS BEACH

_____   _____
_____   _____
_____   _____
_____   _____

Choose a book from your nature library to read today. Document your learning with words and pictures here!

Today's Date: _____

READING TIME

READ A BOOK ABOUT THESE ANIMALS THAT LIVE IN WATER.

Add words and drawings to these pages.

COMMON NAME:

Banana Tree

What is the Scientific Name:

_____

RESEARCH THIS TREE

What can this tree be used for?

_____   _____
_____   _____
_____   _____

Where did it originate?

_____
_____

Where else can it be found?

_____
_____

How did it travel to other parts of the world?

_____
_____

Is this plant in danger of extinction? Why or Why Not?

_____
_____

ANIMALS IN MY REGION

What animal are you learning about?

Common Name:_____

Scientific Name:_____

Draw a Male

Draw a Female

Color the other parts of the world where this animal lives.

COLOR AND RESEARCH
EACH OF THESE REALISTIC DRAWINGS

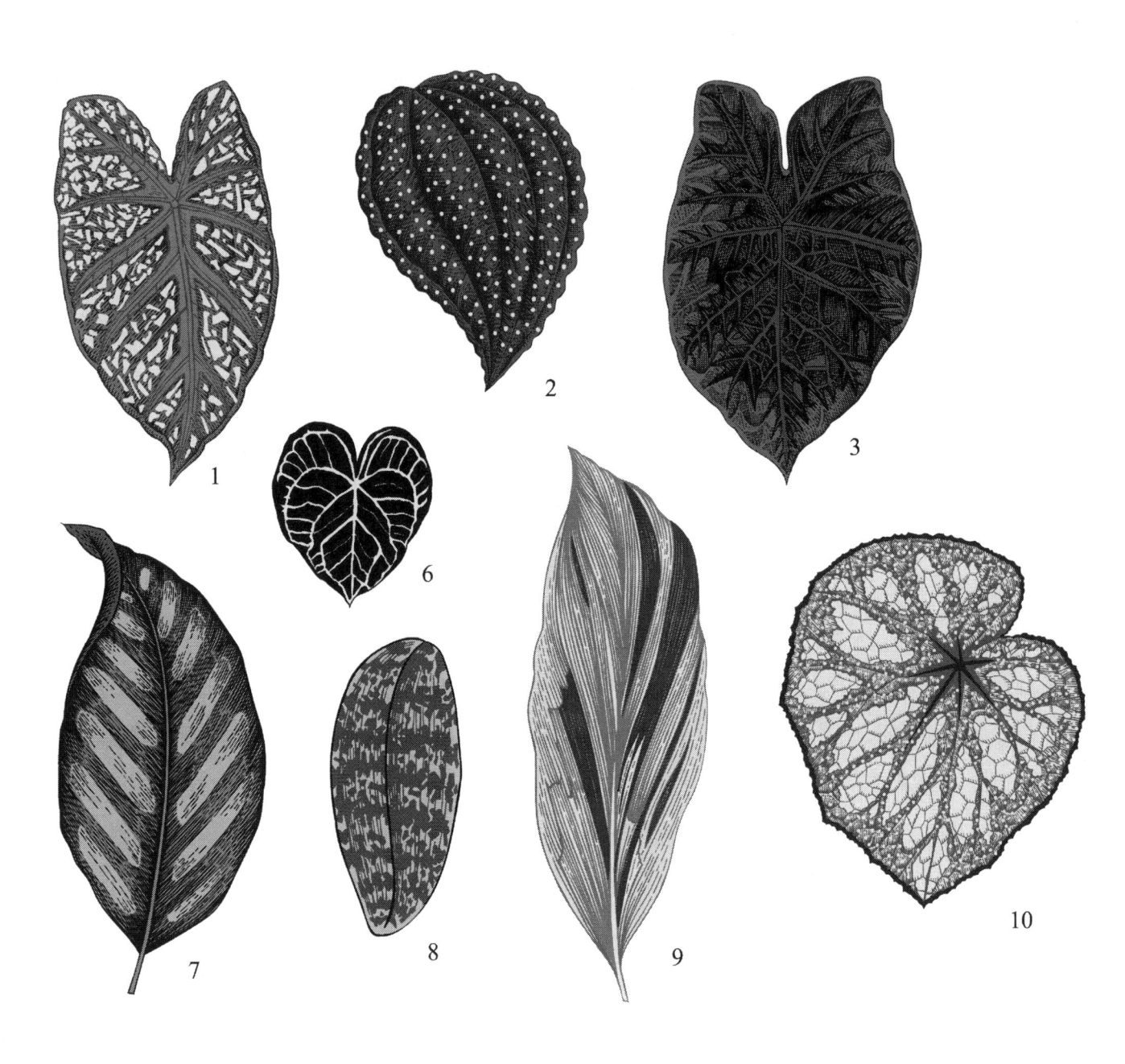

1. Caladium 2. Bertolonia 3. Caladium 4. Calathea 5. Maranta 6. Anthurium 7. Stromanthe

DRAW TWO OF YOUR FAVORITES WITH A FINE POINT BLACK PEN.

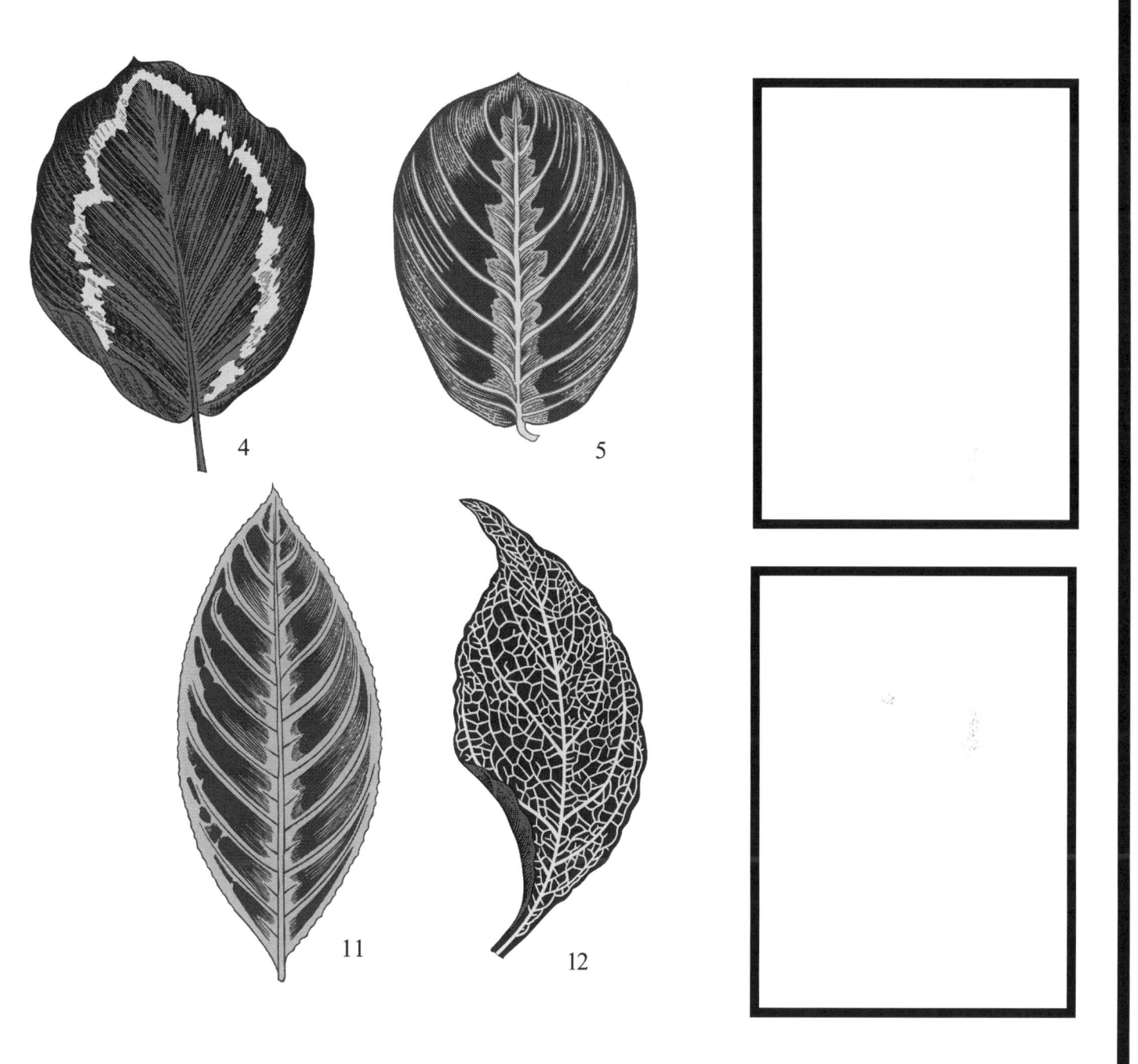

4

5

11

12

. Phalaenopsis Schilleriana   9. Dracaena   10. Begonia Rex   11. Sanchezia Nobilis   12. Fittonia Albivenis

99

STUDY AND COMPARE THESE TWO BEACHES

Beach #1 Sharm El Sheikh, Nabq bay, Egypt

Beach #2 Polulu Beach, Big Island Hawaii, USA

Contact the local wildlife society or nature center to learn more!

DRAW 2 SHELLS THAT CAN BE FOUND ON EACH BEACH.

Beach #1 　　　　　　　　　　　　　　　　Beach #2

LIST 4 LAND ANIMALS THAT CAN BE FOUND AT EACH BEACH

_____　　_____
_____　　_____
_____　　_____
_____　　_____

LIST 4 SEA CREATURES THAT CAN BE FOUND NEAR THIS BEACH

_____　　_____
_____　　_____
_____　　_____
_____　　_____

LIST 4 BIRDS THAT CAN BE SPOTTED NEAR THIS BEACH

_____　　_____
_____　　_____
_____　　_____
_____　　_____

GO ON A HIKE OR NATURE WALK AND DRAW WHAT YOU SEE.

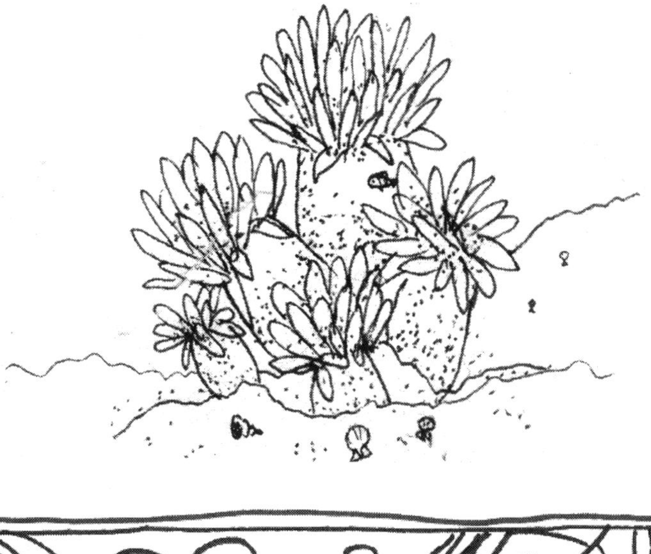

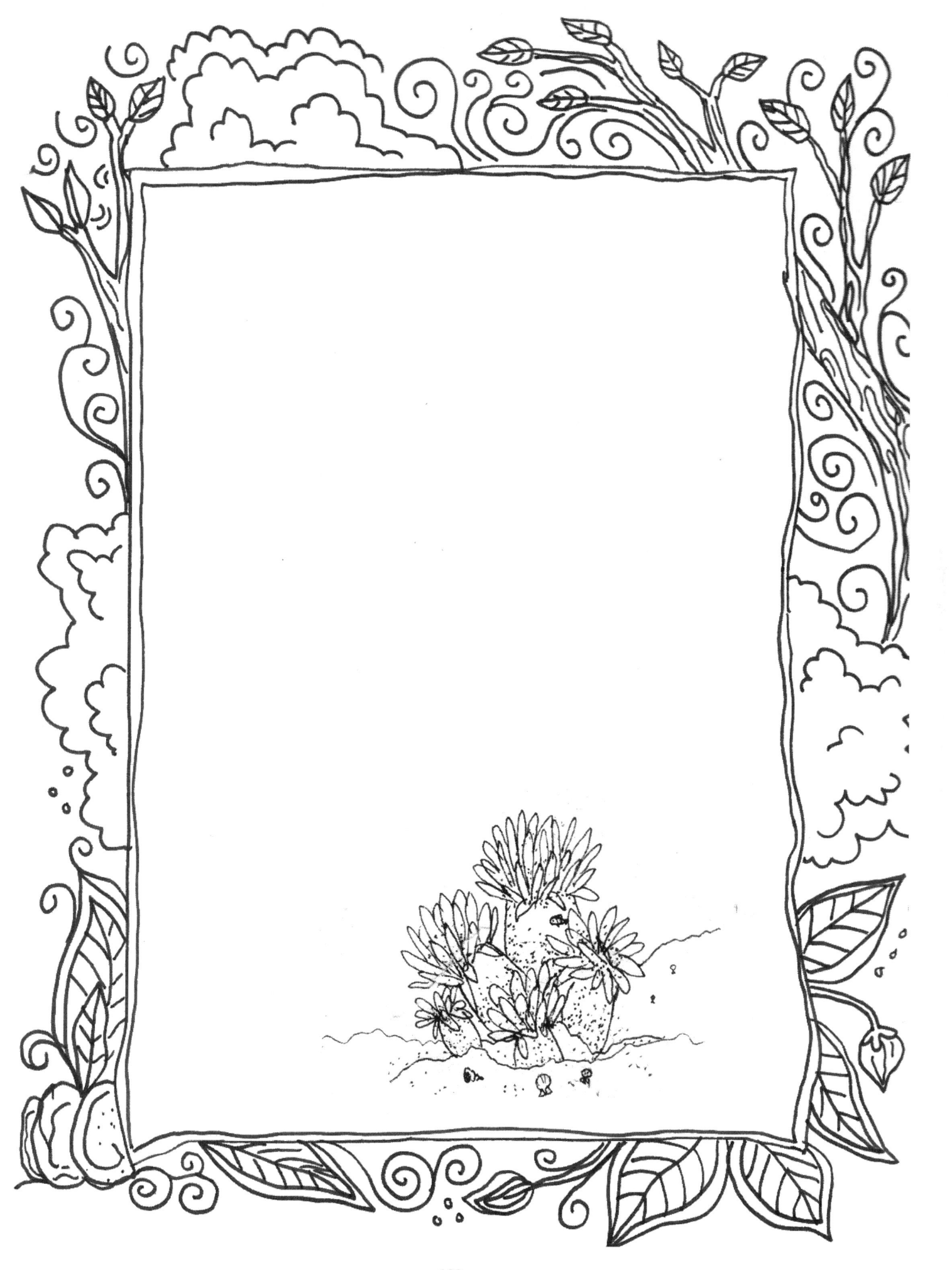

1. COLOR

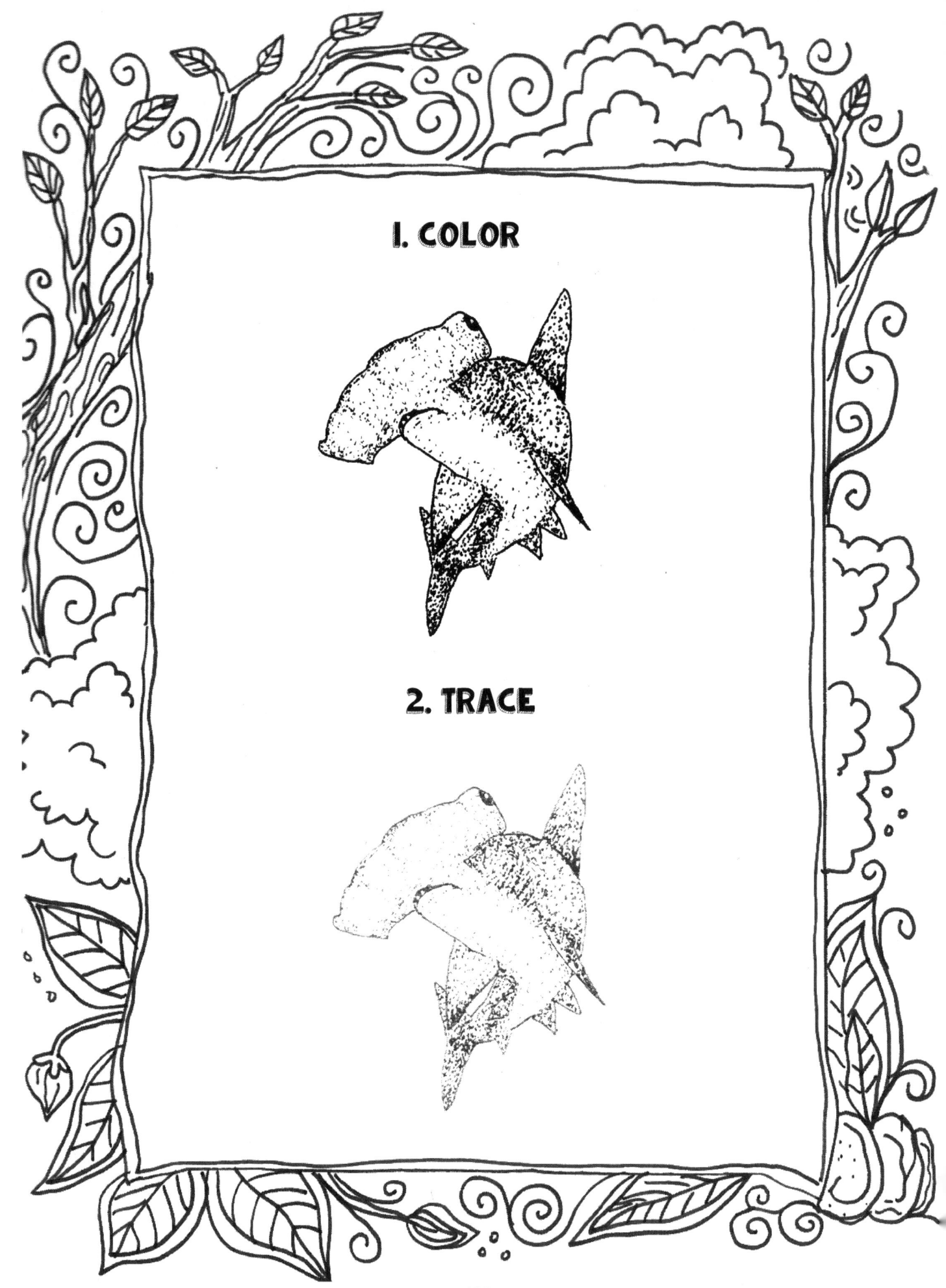

2. TRACE

3. DRAW THE MISSING PART:

4. DRAW THE ANIMAL:

COMMON NAME:

Koa Tree

What is the Scientific Name:

_____

RESEARCH THIS TREE

What can this tree be used for?

_____   _____
_____   _____
_____   _____

Where did it originate?

_____
_____

Where else can it be found?

_____
_____

How did it travel to other parts of the world?

_____
_____

Is this plant in danger of extinction? Why or Why Not?

_____
_____

ANIMALS IN MY REGION

What animal are you learning about?

Common Name:_____

Scientific Name:_____

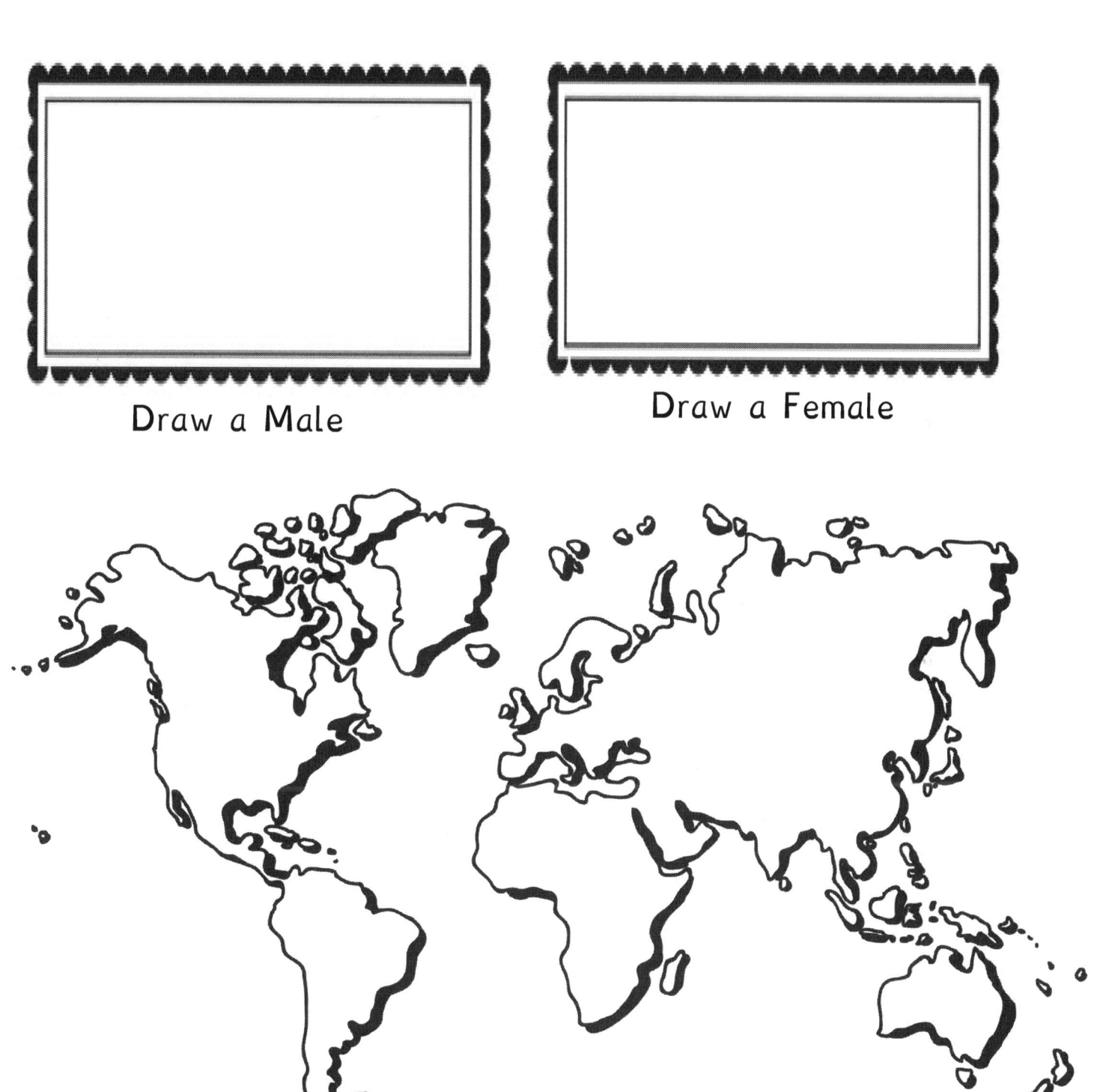

Draw a Male

Draw a Female

Color the other parts of the world where this animal lives.

COLOR AND RESEARCH
EACH OF THESE REALISTIC DRAWINGS

1. & 2. Kelp Laminaria   3. & 6. Rish Moss   4. Bladder Wrack   5. Macrocystis

DRAW TWO OF YOUR FAVORITES WITH A FINE POINT BLACK PEN.

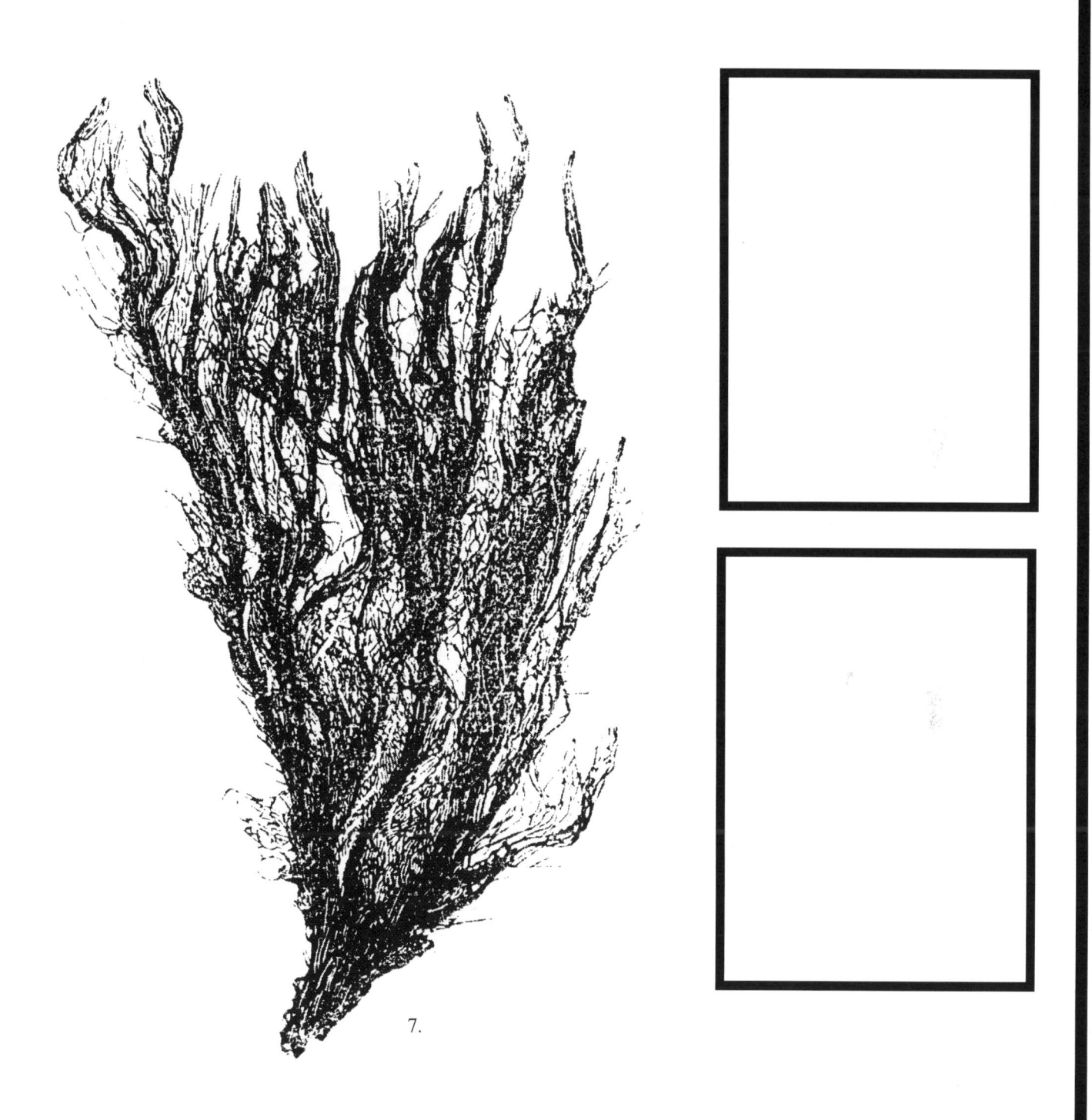

7.

7. Gutweed

STUDY AND COMPARE THESE TWO BEACHES

Beach #1   Twelve Apostles, Australia

Beach #2   Acadia National Park, Maine, USA

Contact the local wildlife society or nature center to learn more!

DRAW 2 SHELLS THAT CAN BE FOUND ON EACH BEACH.

Beach #1　　　　　　　　　　　　　　　Beach #2

LIST 4 LAND ANIMALS THAT CAN BE FOUND AT EACH BEACH

_____   _____
_____   _____
_____   _____
_____   _____

LIST 4 SEA CREATURES THAT CAN BE FOUND NEAR THIS BEACH

_____   _____
_____   _____
_____   _____
_____   _____

LIST 4 BIRDS THAT CAN BE SPOTTED NEAR THIS BEACH

_____   _____
_____   _____
_____   _____
_____   _____

Choose a book from your nature library to read today. Document your learning with words and pictures here!

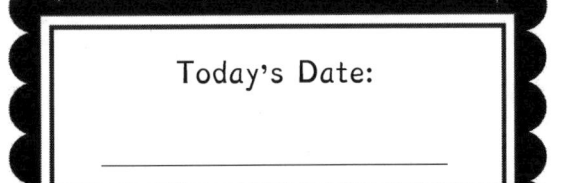

Today's Date:

READING TIME

**DRAW A PICTURE FROM ONE OF YOUR
NATURE BOOKS ABOUT DANGEROUS ANIMALS**

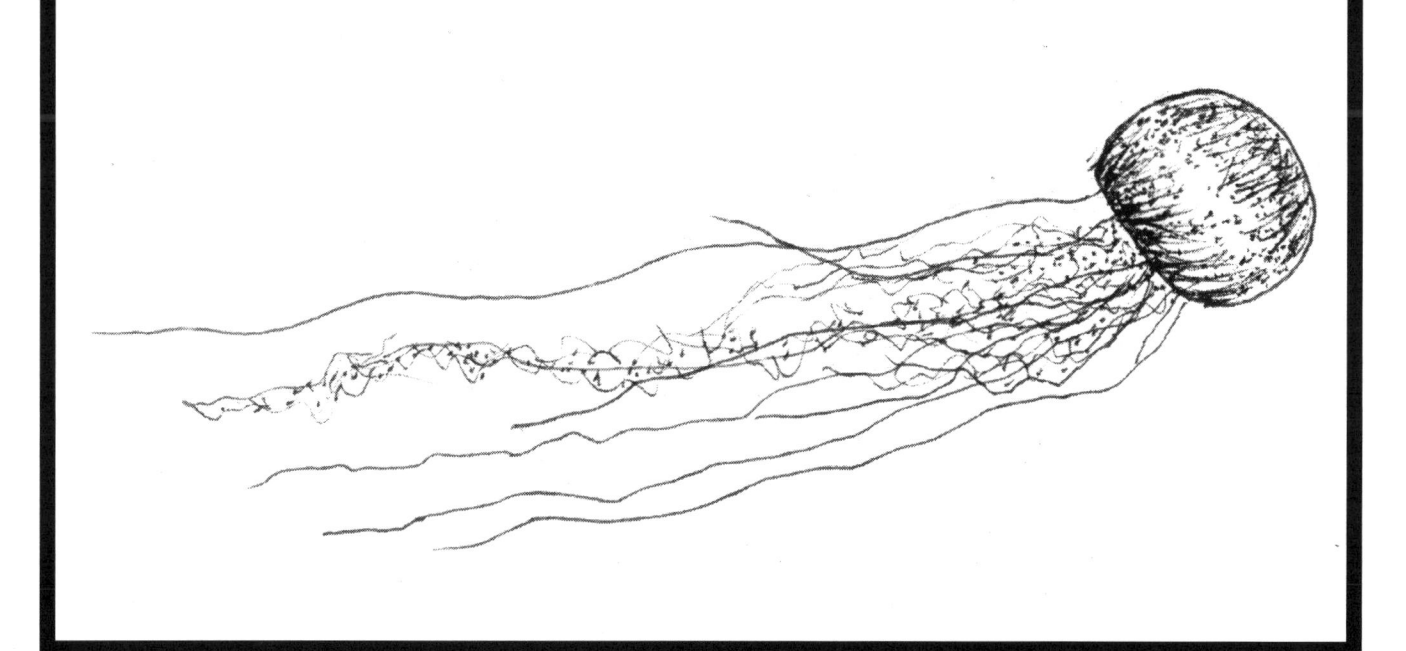

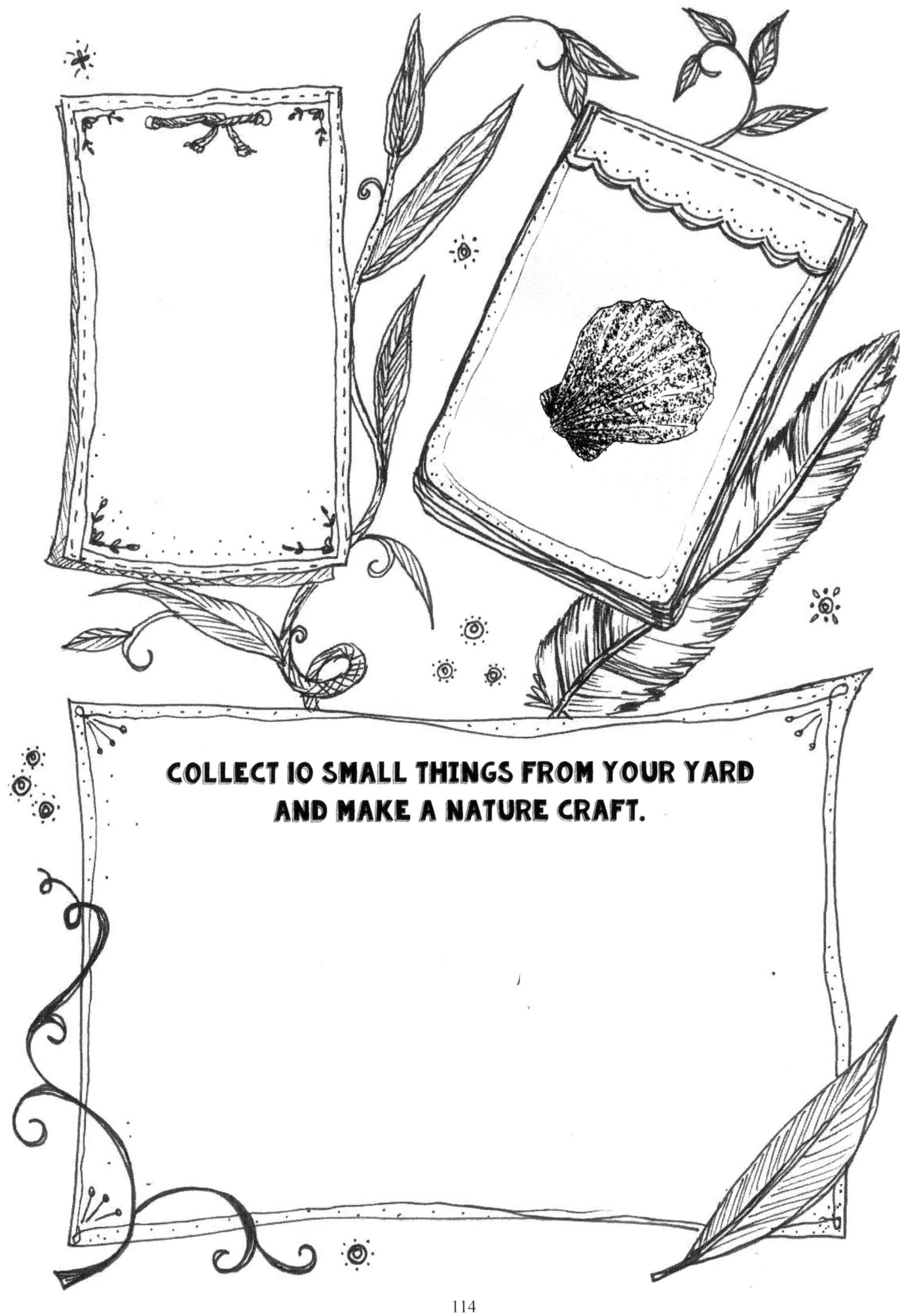

COLLECT 10 SMALL THINGS FROM YOUR YARD AND MAKE A NATURE CRAFT.

DRAW SMALL THINGS YOU SEE OUTSIDE

DRAW A MAP OF YOUR FAVORITE BEACH AREA

DRAW A MAP OF YOUR YARD

1. COLOR

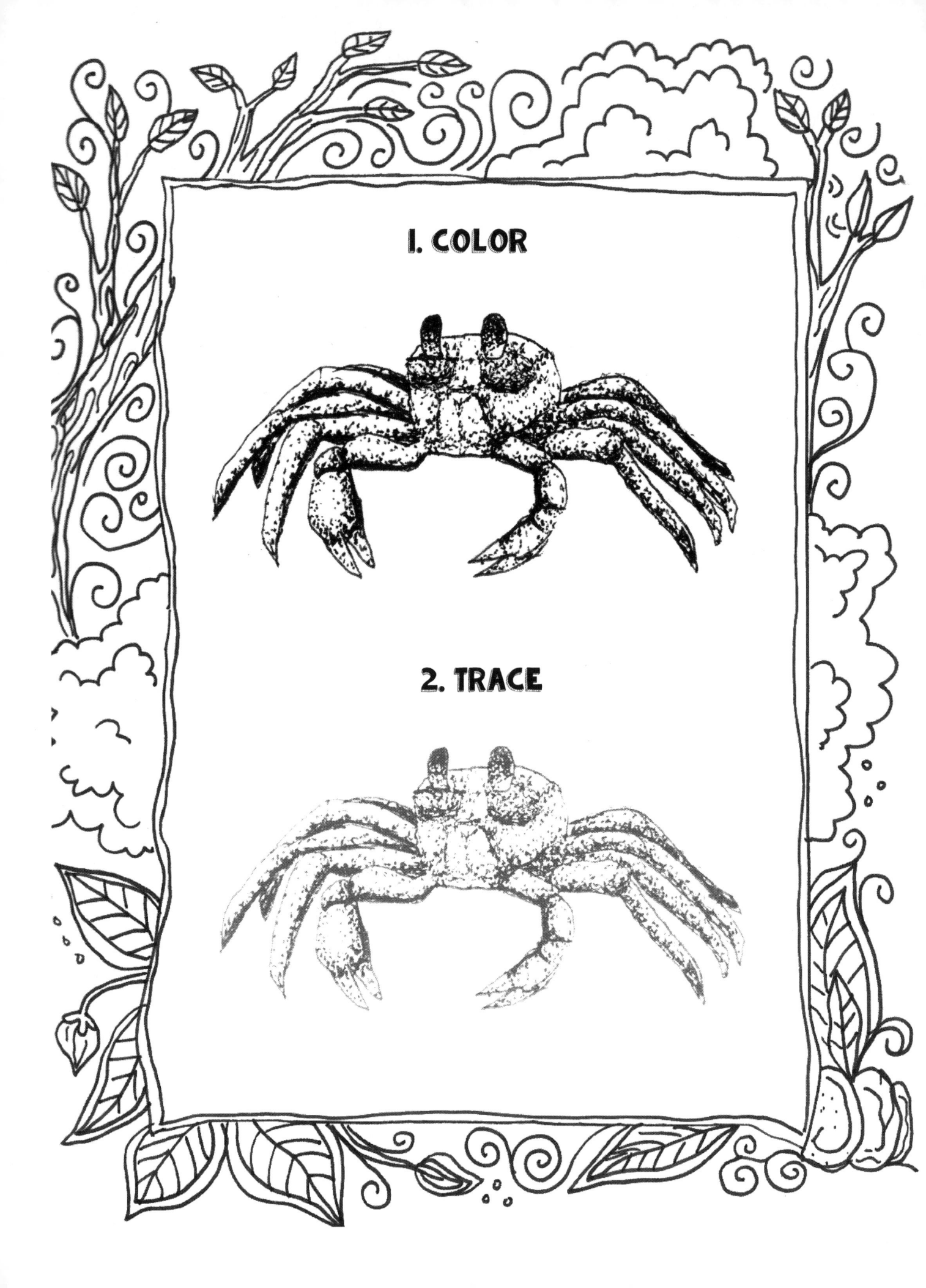

2. TRACE

3. DRAW THE MISSING PART:

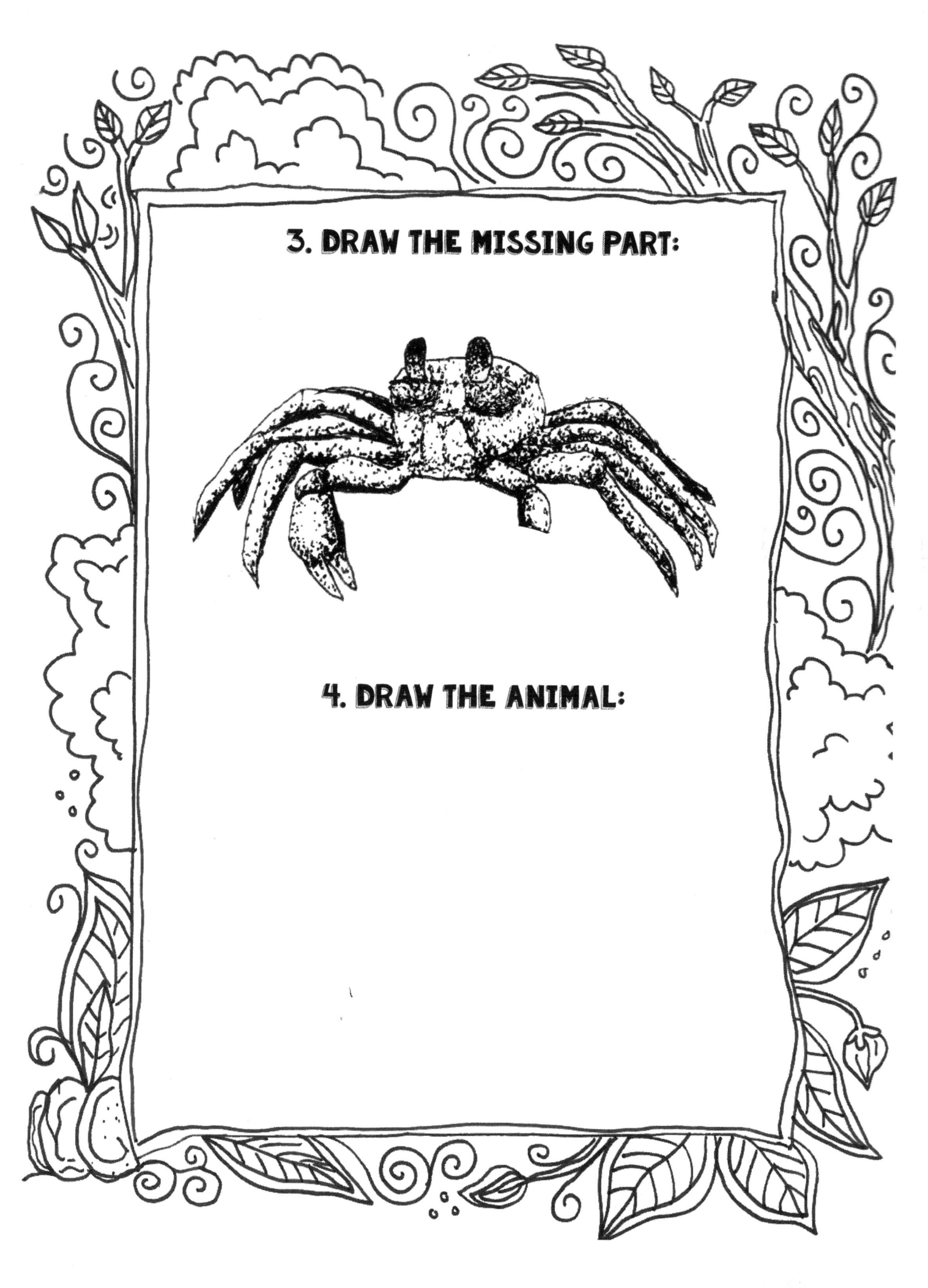

4. DRAW THE ANIMAL:

COMMON NAME:

Palm Tree

What is the Scientific Name:

_____

RESEARCH THIS TREE

What can this tree be used for?

_____   _____
_____   _____
_____   _____

Where did it originate?

_____
_____

Where else can it be found?

_____
_____

How did it travel to other parts of the world?

_____
_____

Is this plant in danger of extinction? Why or Why Not?

_____
_____

ANIMALS IN MY REGION

What animal are you learning about?

Common Name:_____

Scientific Name:_____

Draw a Male

Draw a Female

Color the other parts of the world where this animal lives.

COLOR AND RESEARCH EACH OF THESE REALISTIC DRAWINGS

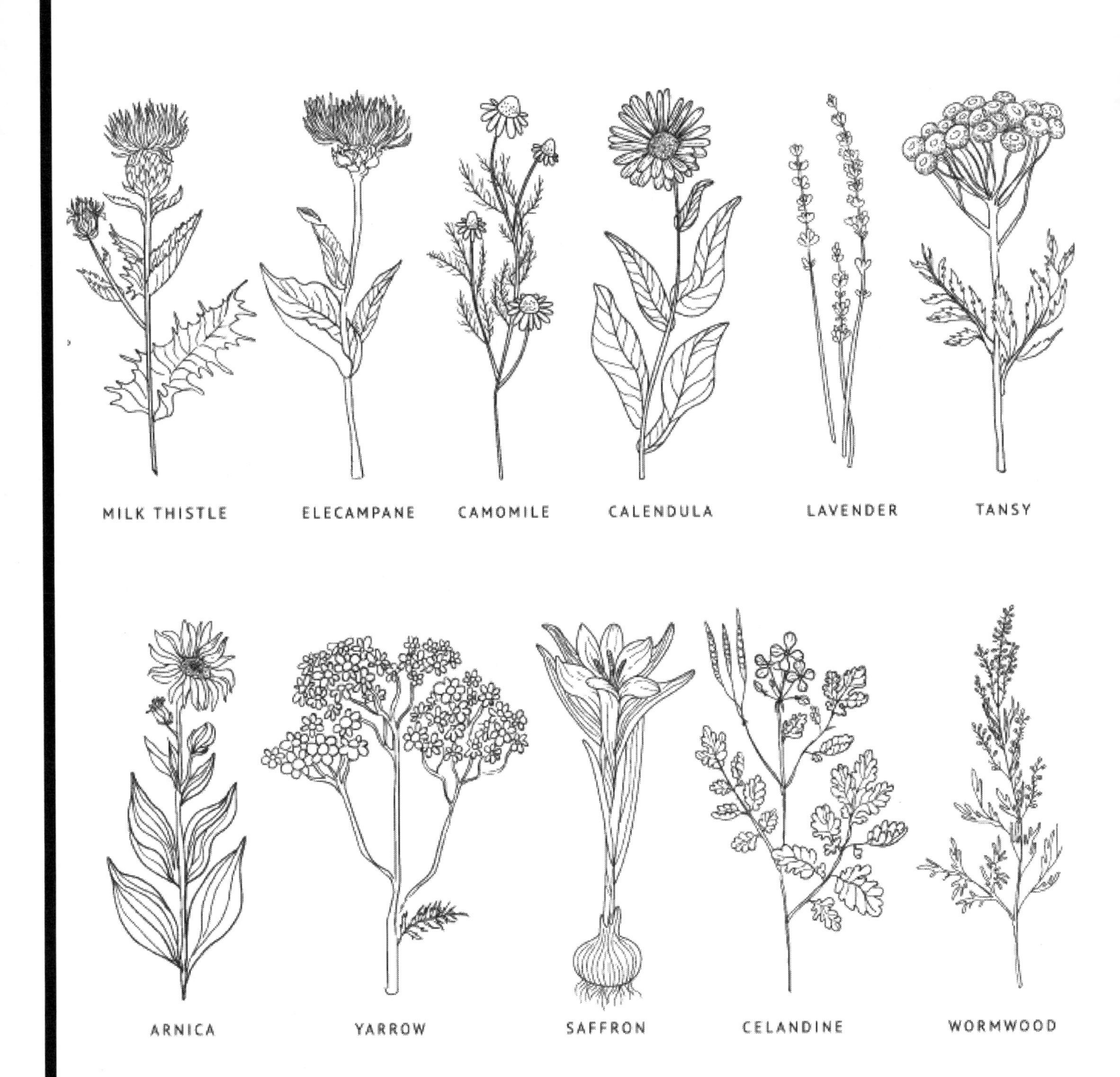

MILK THISTLE   ELECAMPANE   CAMOMILE   CALENDULA   LAVENDER   TANSY

ARNICA   YARROW   SAFFRON   CELANDINE   WORMWOOD

DRAW TWO OF YOUR FAVORITES WITH A FINE POINT BLACK PEN.

ST. JOHN'S WORT VALERIAN DANDELION SAGE

NETTLE CLOVER PLANTAIN

STUDY AND COMPARE THESE TWO BEACHES

Beach #1 Coast Line, Shenzhen, China

Beach #2 Walnut Beach, Milford, Connecticut, USA

Contact the local wildlife society or nature center to learn more!

DRAW 2 SHELLS THAT CAN BE FOUND ON EACH BEACH.

Beach #1   Beach #2

LIST 4 LAND ANIMALS THAT CAN BE FOUND AT EACH BEACH

_____   _____
_____   _____
_____   _____
_____   _____

LIST 4 SEA CREATURES THAT CAN BE FOUND NEAR THIS BEACH

_____   _____
_____   _____
_____   _____
_____   _____

LIST 4 BIRDS THAT CAN BE SPOTTED NEAR THIS BEACH

_____   _____
_____   _____
_____   _____
_____   _____

ADD YOUR OWN ART TO FINISH THE PICTURE

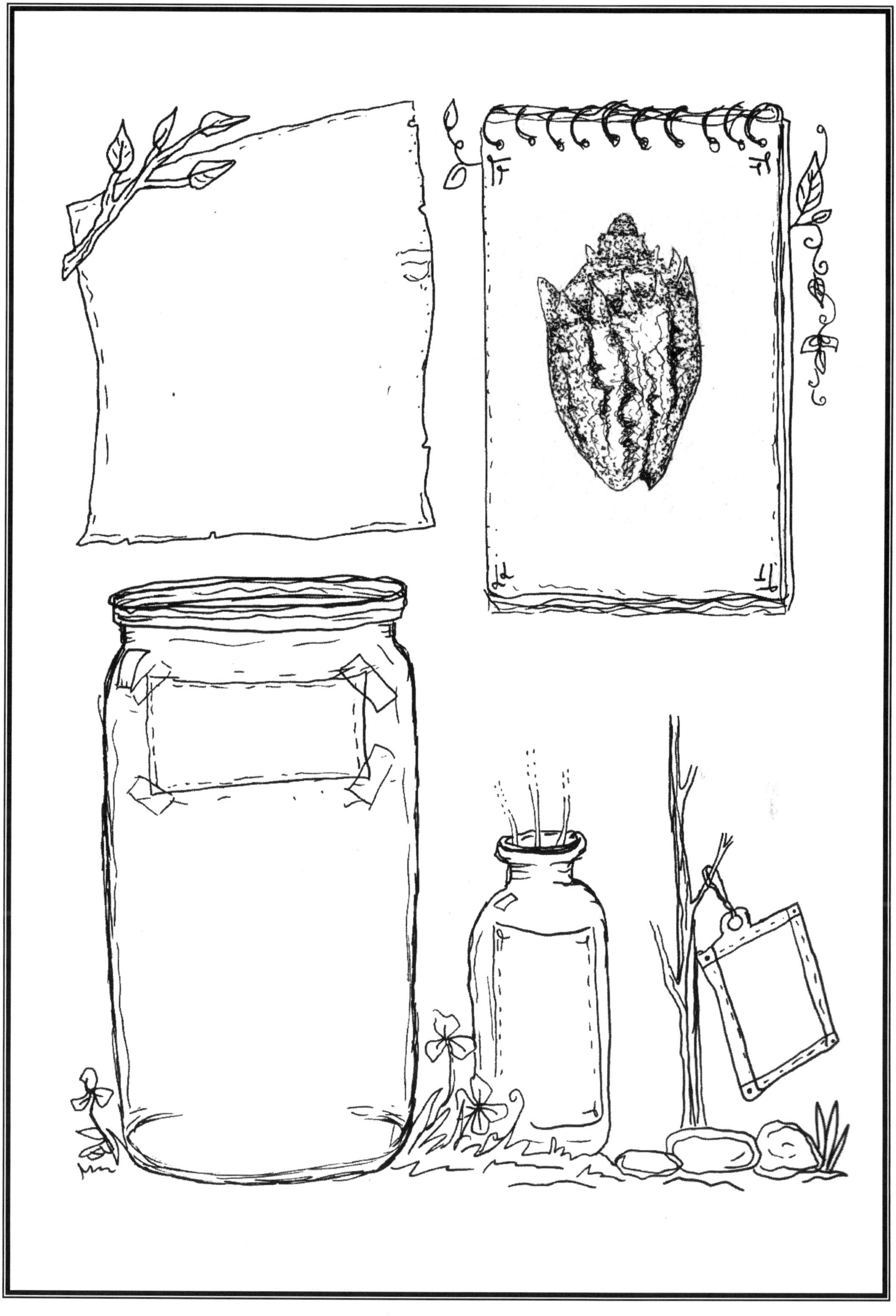

COMMON NAME:

Mangrove Tree

What is the Scientific Name:

_____

RESEARCH THIS TREE

What can this tree be used for?

_____   _____
_____   _____
_____   _____

Where did it originate?

_____
_____

Where else can it be found?

_____
_____

How did it travel to other parts of the world?

_____
_____

Is this plant in danger of extinction? Why or Why Not?

_____
_____

ANIMALS IN MY REGION

What animal are you learning about?

Common Name:_____

Scientific Name:_____

Draw a Male

Draw a Female

Color the other parts of the world where this animal lives.

COLOR AND RESEARCH EACH OF THESE REALISTIC DRAWINGS

1.

2.

3.

1. Mango 2. Papaya 3. Coconut

DRAW TWO OF YOUR FAVORITES WITH A FINE POINT BLACK PEN.

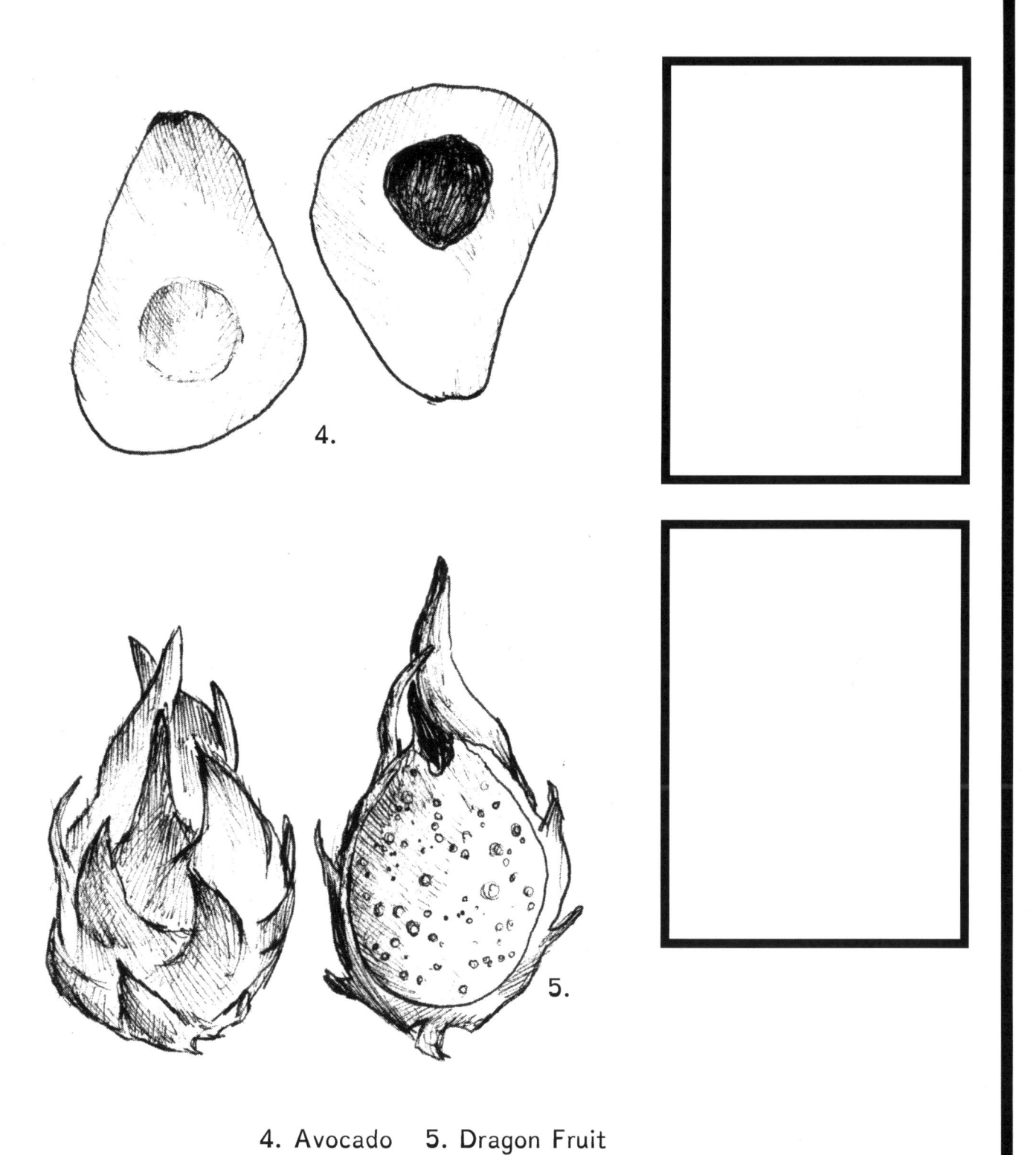

4.

4. Avocado   5. Dragon Fruit

STUDY AND COMPARE THESE TWO BEACHES

Beach #1 Ipanema beach in Rio de Janeiro. Brazil.

Beach #2 Rye, New Hampshire, USA

Contact the local wildlife society or nature center to learn more!

DRAW 2 SHELLS THAT CAN BE FOUND ON EACH BEACH.

Beach #1 Beach #2

LIST 4 LAND ANIMALS THAT CAN BE FOUND AT EACH BEACH

LIST 4 SEA CREATURES THAT CAN BE FOUND NEAR THIS BEACH

LIST 4 BIRDS THAT CAN BE SPOTTED NEAR THIS BEACH

Choose a book from your nature library to read today. Document your learning with words and pictures here!

Today's Date:
_____

READING TIME

DRAW A PICTURE FROM ONE OF YOUR NATURE BOOKS ABOUT ANIMALS THAT LIVE IN SHELLS

USE A CAMERA
TO TAKE PICTURES OF NATURE

Print your photos and place them here:

COMMON NAME:

Royal Poinciana Tree

What is the Scientific Name:

_____

RESEARCH THIS TREE

What can this tree be used for?

_____   _____
_____   _____
_____   _____

Where did it originate?

_____
_____

Where else can it be found?

_____
_____

How did it travel to other parts of the world?

_____
_____

Is this plant in danger of extinction? Why or Why Not?

_____
_____

ANIMALS IN MY REGION

What animal are you learning about?

Common Name:_____

Scientific Name:_____

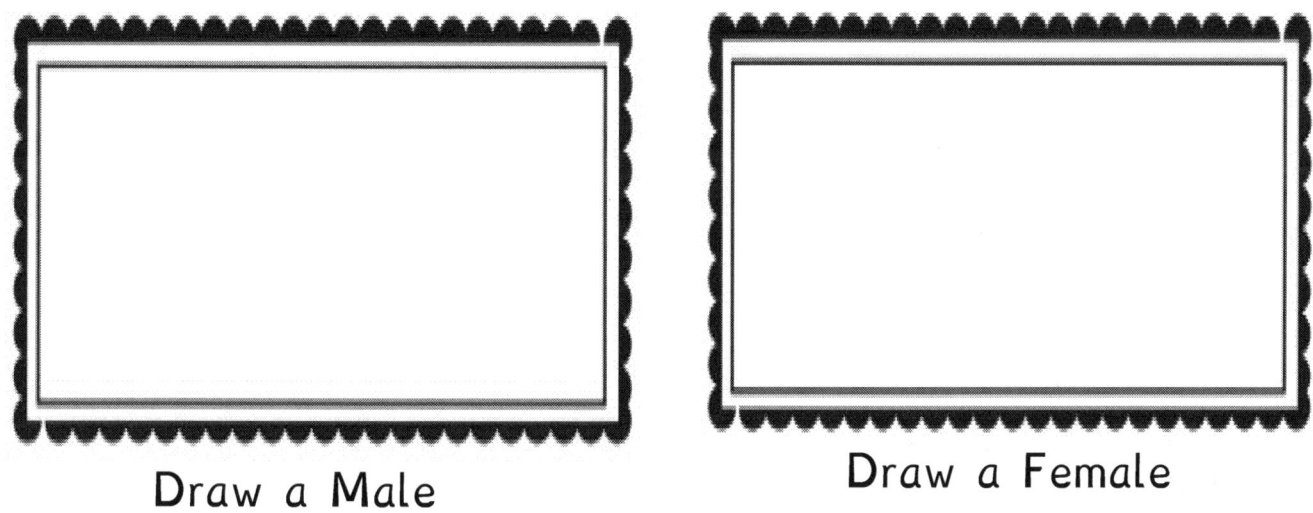

Draw a Male

Draw a Female

Color the other parts of the world where this animal lives.

COLOR AND RESEARCH
EACH OF THESE REALISTIC DRAWINGS

1.

2.

3.

1. Ōʻū   **2.** Aeʻo   **3.** Puaiohi

DRAW TWO OF YOUR FAVORITES WITH A FINE POINT BLACK PEN.

4.

5.

4. Kāmaʻo   5. Hawaii mamo

STUDY AND COMPARE THESE TWO BEACHES

Beach #1 Sironit beach, Netanya, Israel.

Beach #2 Sandbridge beach in Virginia beach, Virginia, USA

Contact the local wildlife society or nature center to learn more!

DRAW 2 SHELLS THAT CAN BE FOUND ON EACH BEACH.

Beach #1   Beach #2

LIST 4 LAND ANIMALS THAT CAN BE FOUND AT EACH BEACH

LIST 4 SEA CREATURES THAT CAN BE FOUND NEAR THIS BEACH

LIST 4 BIRDS THAT CAN BE SPOTTED NEAR THIS BEACH

COLLECT 10 SMALL THINGS FROM NATURE AND MAKE A NATURE CRAFT.

FIND AND COLOR IN THE HIDDEN OBJECTS

1. COLOR

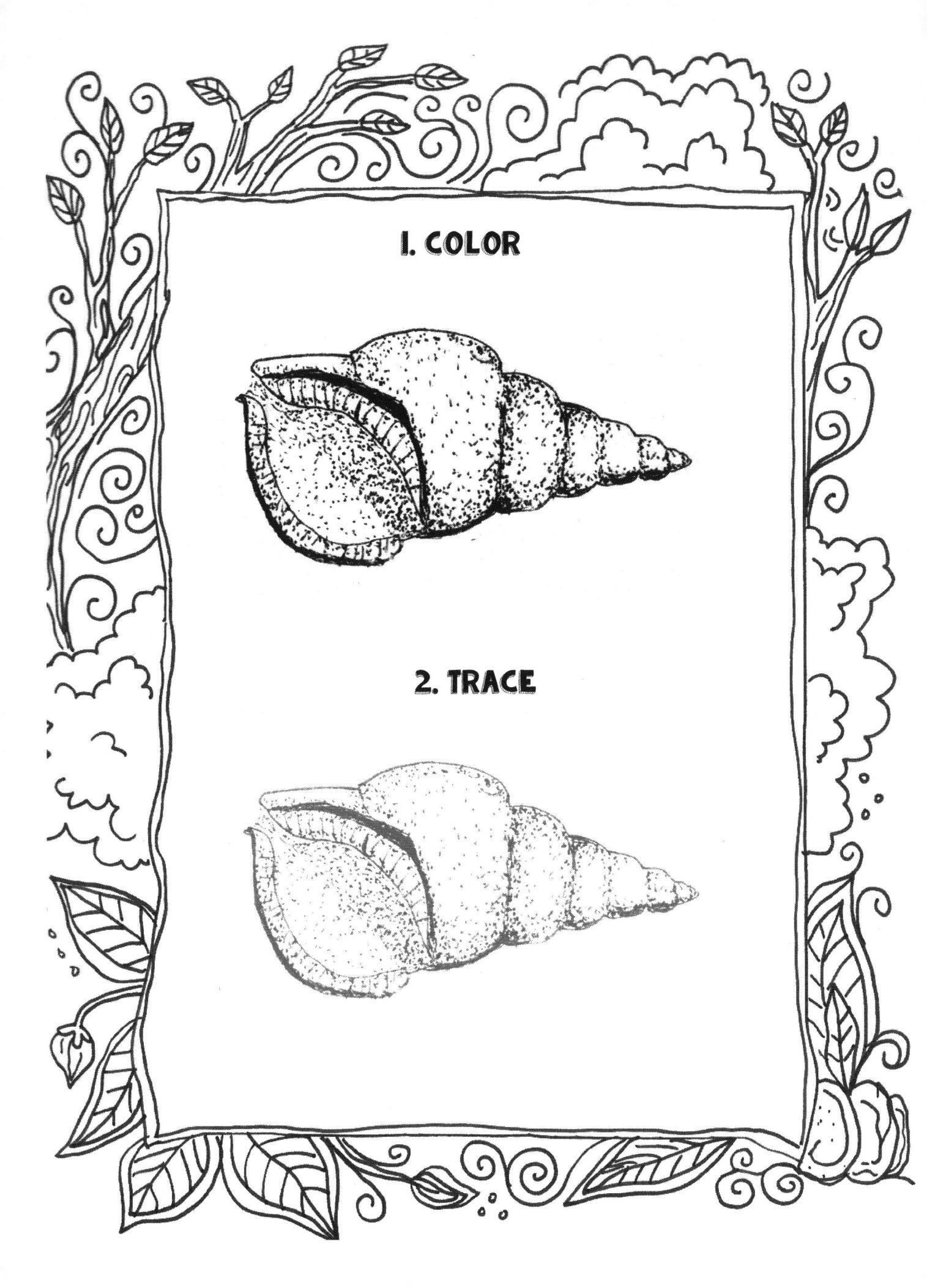

2. TRACE

3. DRAW THE MISSING PART:

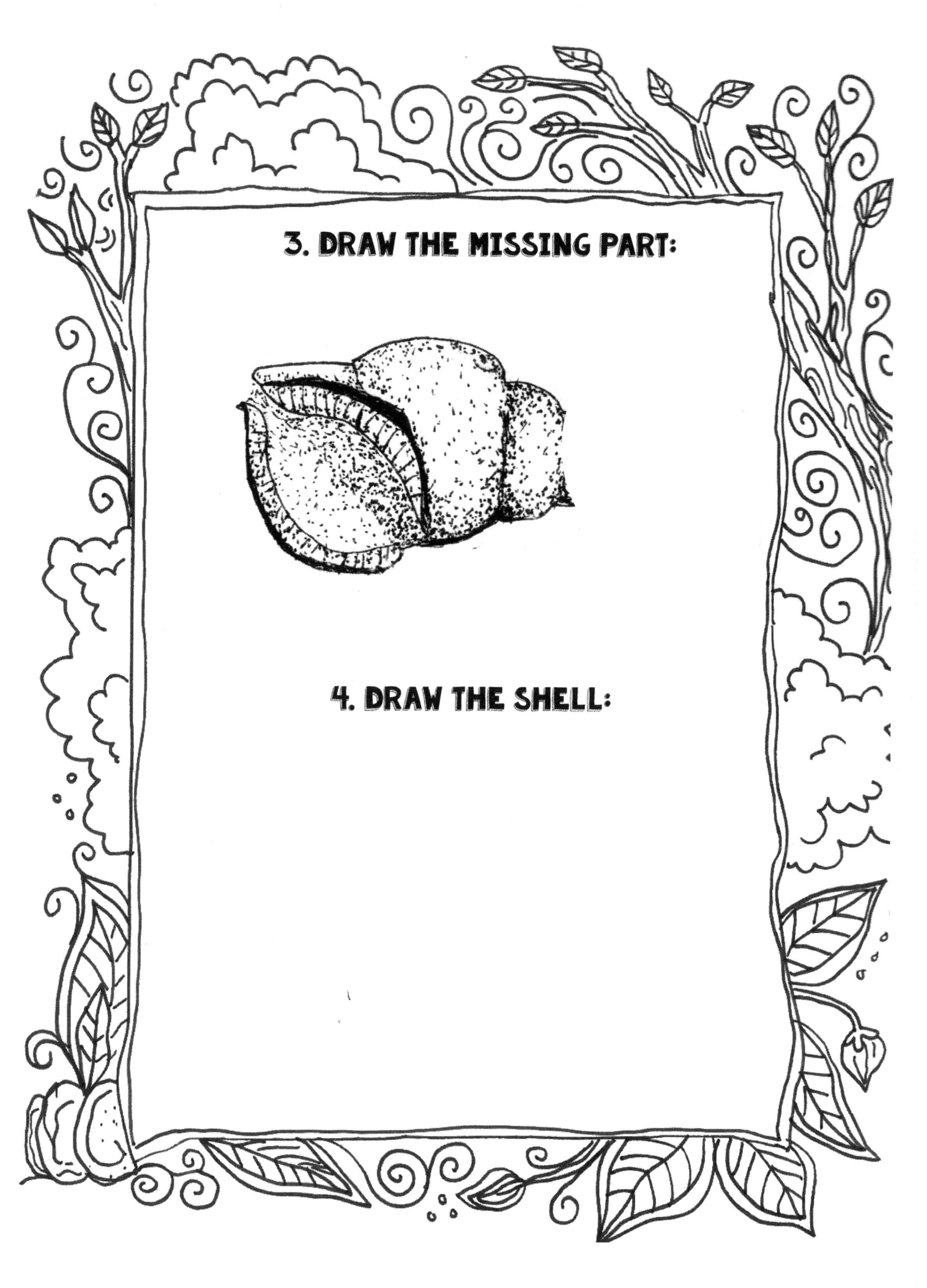

4. DRAW THE SHELL:

LOOK IN A BOOK & DRAW A SHELL IN EACH BOX

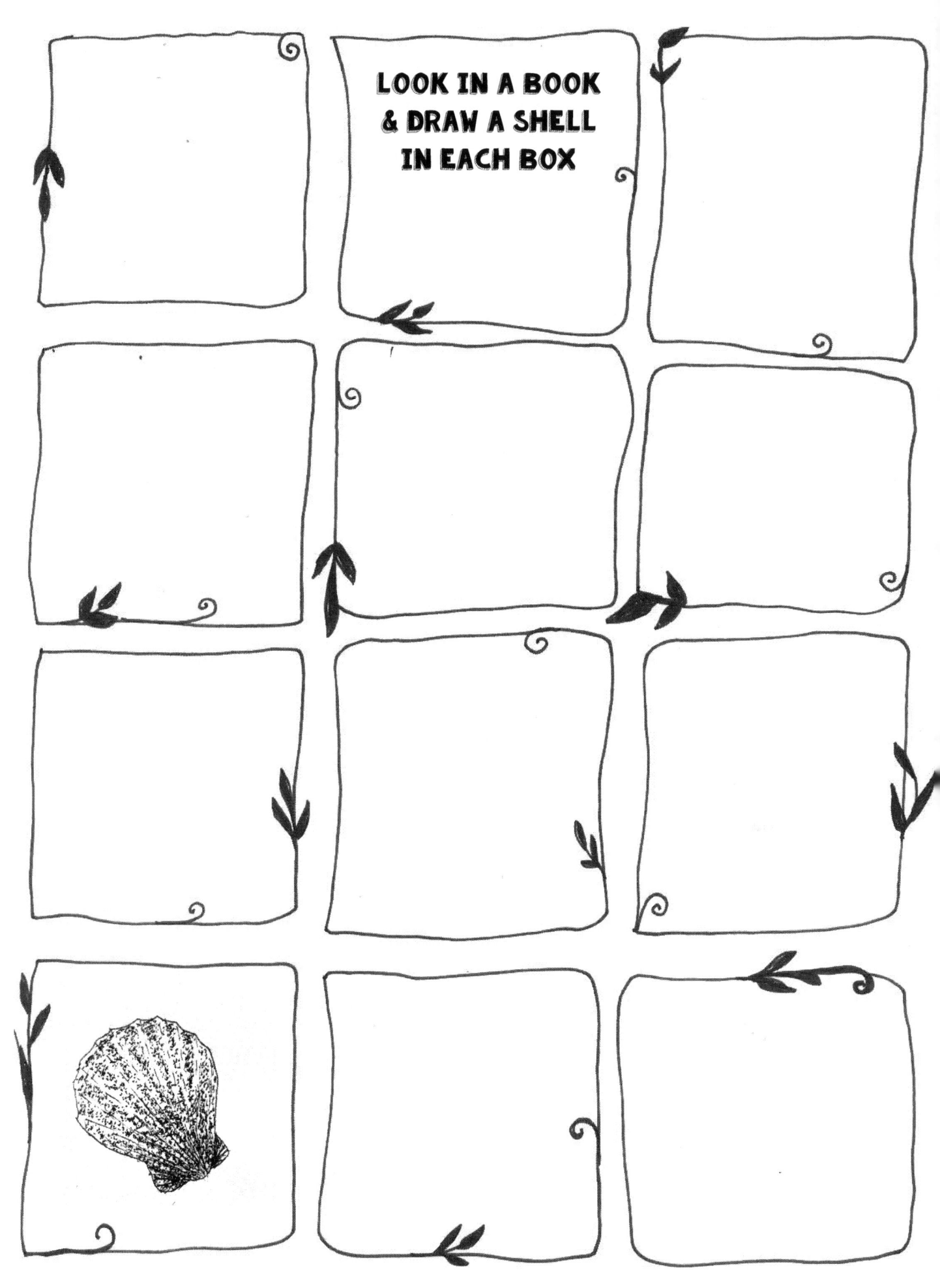

LOOK IN A BOOK & DRAW A BUTTERFLY IN EACH BOX

Choose a book from your nature library to read today. Document your learning with words and pictures here!

READING TIME

Today's Date: _____

COLOR ME
DRAW MY FOOD & HABITAT

DRAW A PICTURE OF YOUR FAVORITE ANIMAL

RESEARCH YOUR FAVORITE ANIMAL

COLOR AND RESEARCH EACH OF THESE REALISTIC DRAWINGS

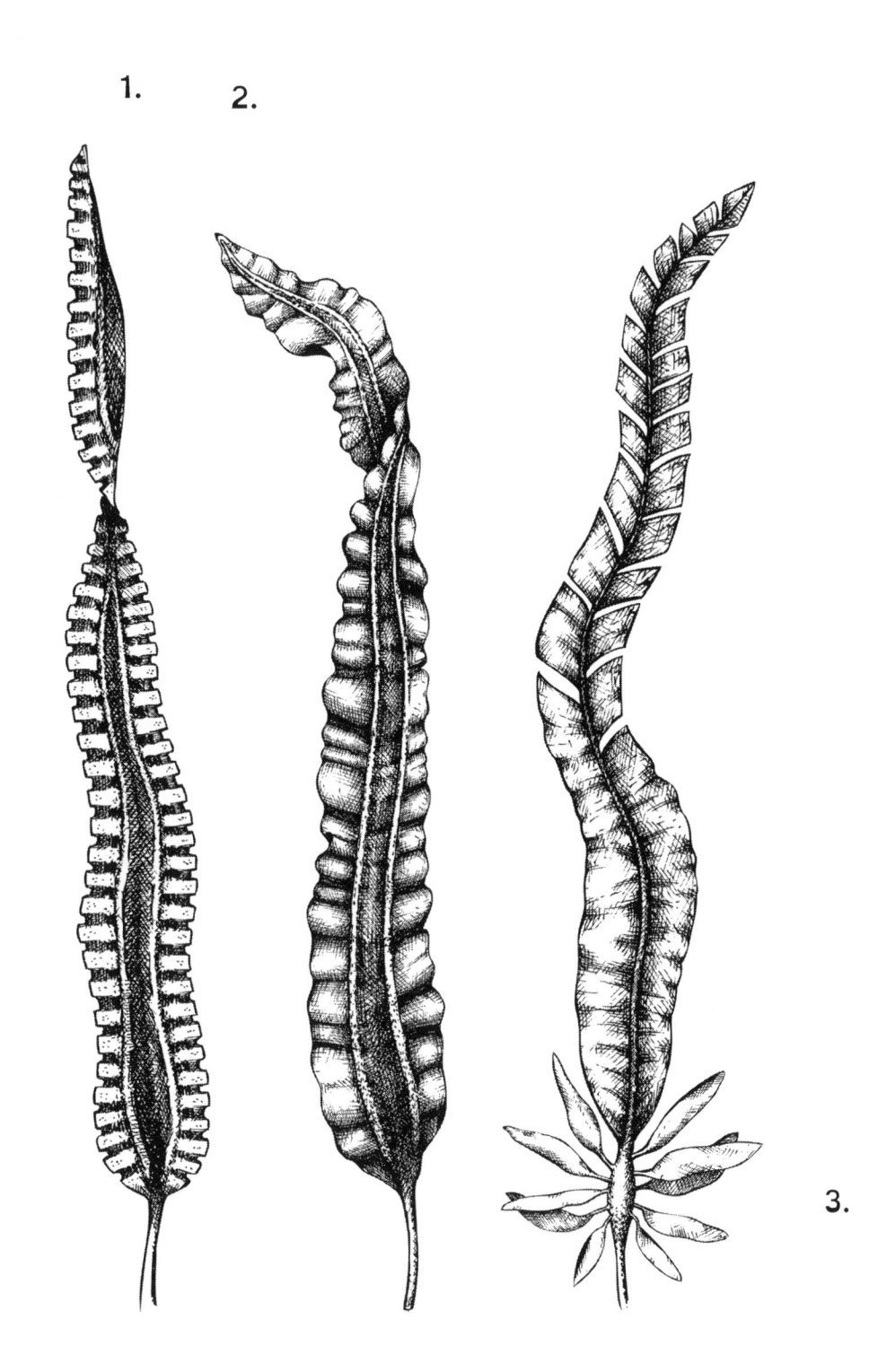

1.
2.

3.

1. Sweet Sea Tangle, 2. Japan Kelp, 3. Alaria

DRAW TWO OF YOUR FAVORITES WITH A FINE POINT BLACK PEN.

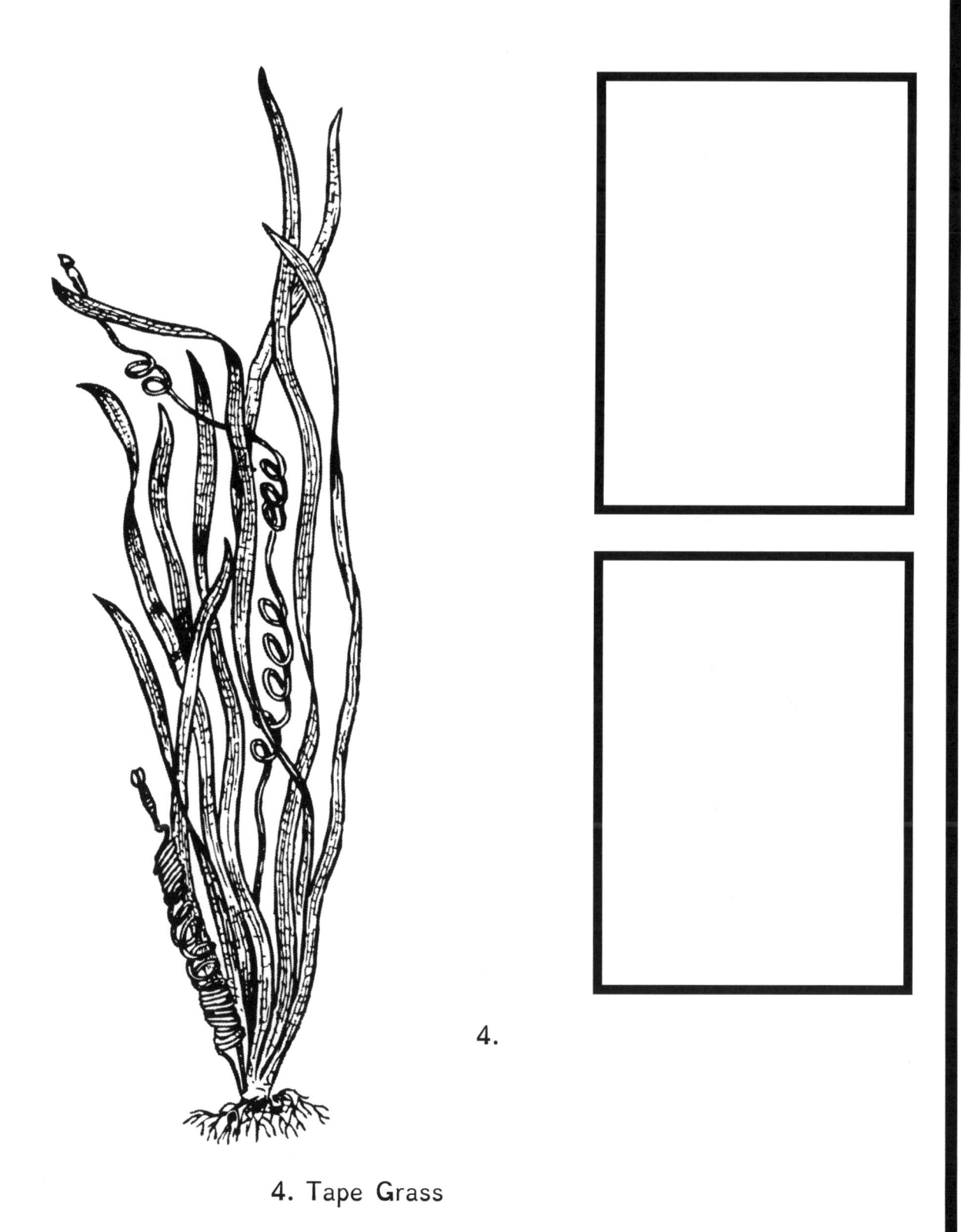

4.

4. Tape Grass

COMMON NAME:

Plumeria

What is the Scientific Name:

_____

RESEARCH THIS PLANT

What can this plant be used for?

_____ _____
_____ _____
_____ _____

Where did it originate?

_____
_____

Where else can it be found?

_____
_____

How did it travel to other parts of the world?

_____
_____

Is this plant in danger of extinction? Why or Why Not?

_____
_____

ANIMALS IN MY REGION

What animal are you learning about?

Common Name:_____

Scientific Name:_____

Draw a Male

Draw a Female

Color the other parts of the world where this animal lives.

STUDY AND COMPARE THESE TWO BEACHES

Beach #1 Dunquin bay, Ireland

Beach #2 Cannon Beach, Oregon State, USA.

Contact the local wildlife society or nature center to learn more!

DRAW 2 SHELLS THAT CAN BE FOUND ON EACH BEACH.

Beach #1   Beach #2

LIST 4 LAND ANIMALS THAT CAN BE FOUND AT EACH BEACH

_____   _____
_____   _____
_____   _____
_____   _____

LIST 4 SEA CREATURES THAT CAN BE FOUND NEAR THIS BEACH

_____   _____
_____   _____
_____   _____
_____   _____

LIST 4 BIRDS THAT CAN BE SPOTTED NEAR THIS BEACH

_____   _____
_____   _____
_____   _____
_____   _____

COLOR AND RESEARCH EACH OF THESE REALISTIC DRAWINGS

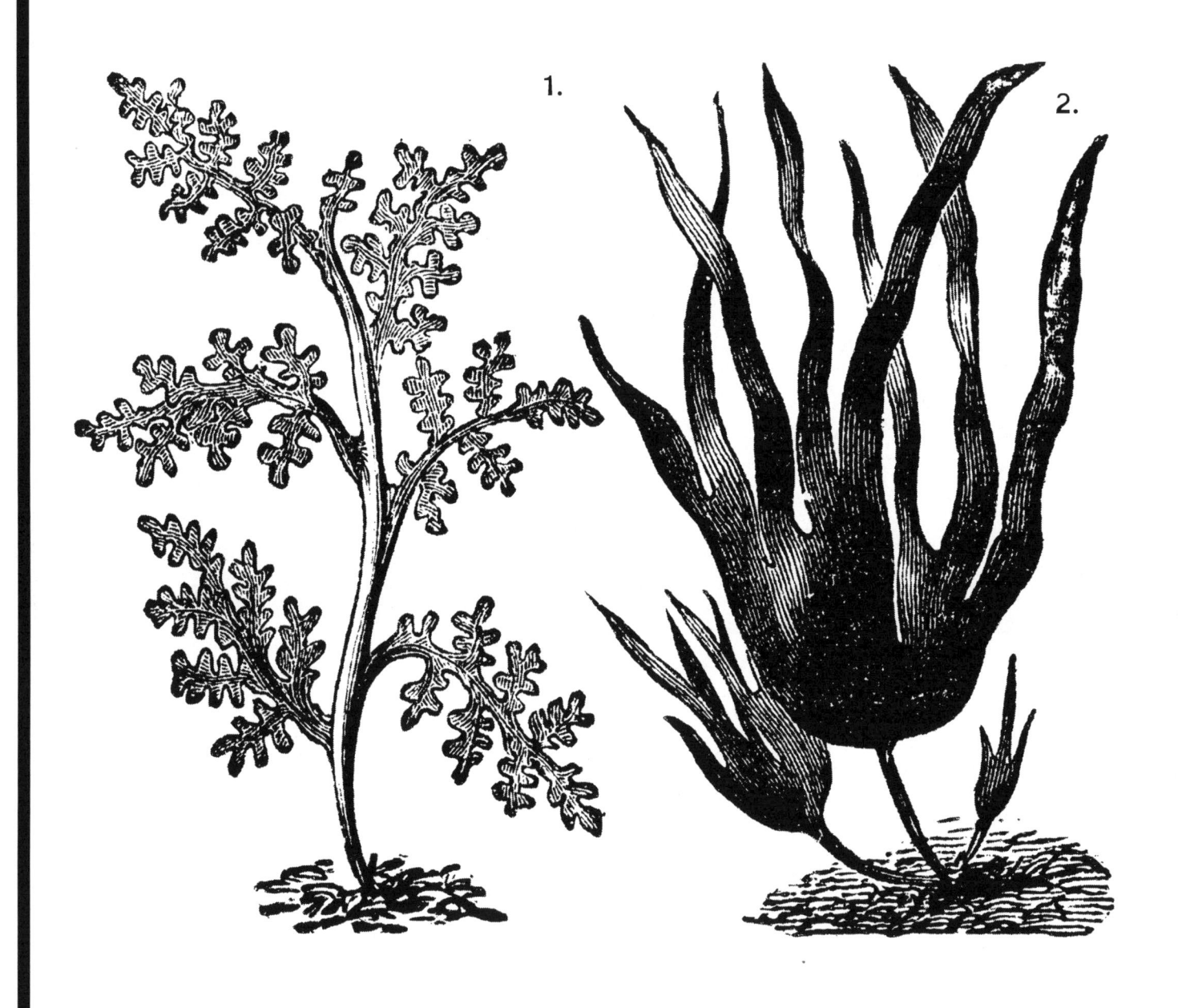

1.

2.

1. Pepper dulse   2. Oarweed

DRAW TWO OF YOUR FAVORITES WITH A FINE POINT BLACK PEN.

3. Sea Squill

GO OUTSIDE AND DRAW THE SKY

NATURE NOTES, QUOTES AND POETRY

COMMON NAME:
Dahila

What is the Scientific Name:

_____

RESEARCH THIS PLANT

What can this plant be used for?

_____   _____
_____   _____
_____   _____

Where did it originate?

_____
_____

Where else can it be found?

_____
_____

How did it travel to other parts of the world?

_____
_____

Is this plant in danger of extinction? Why or Why Not?

_____
_____

ANIMALS IN MY REGION

What animal are you learning about?

Common Name:_____

Scientific Name:_____

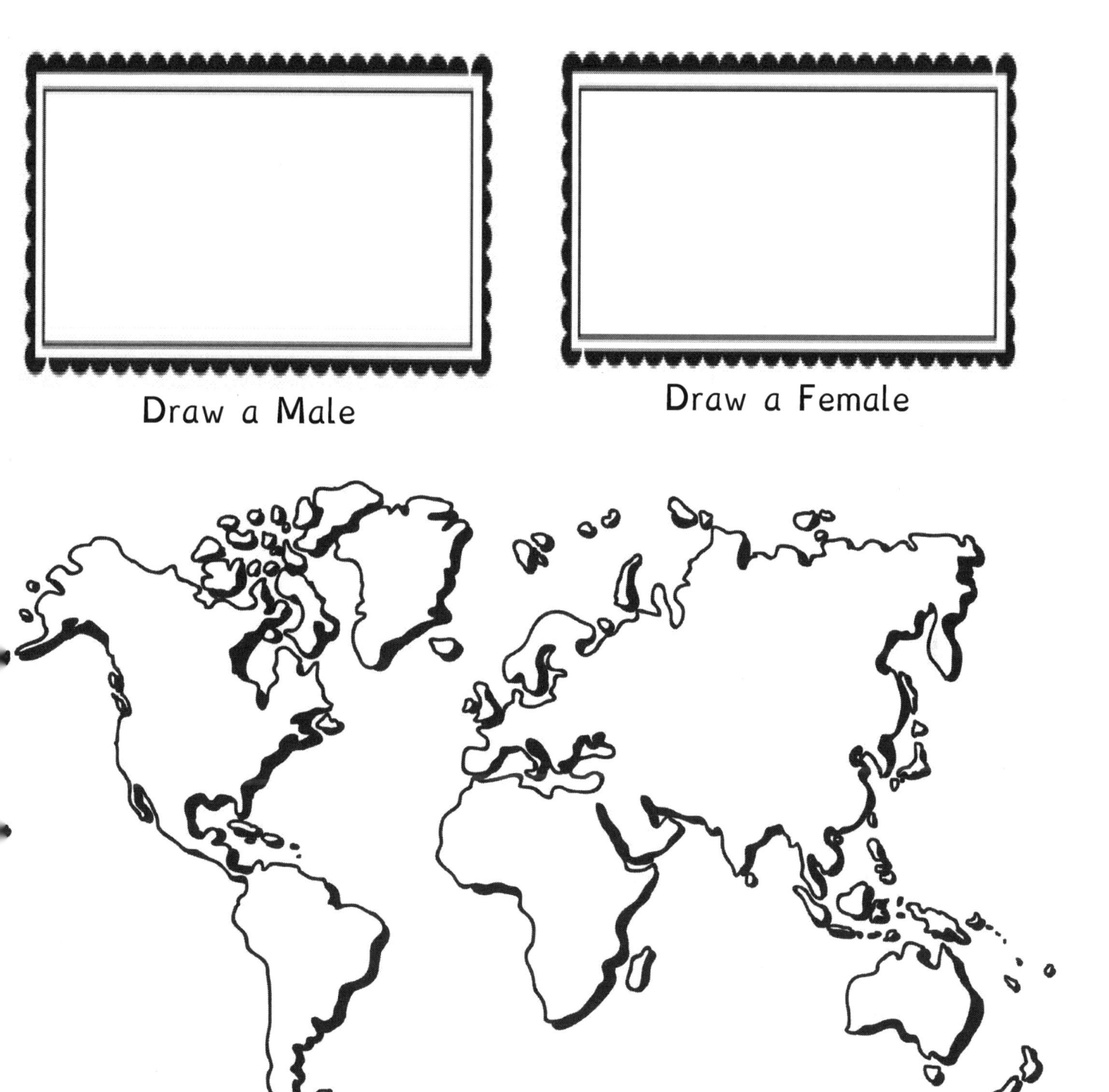

Draw a Male

Draw a Female

Color the other parts of the world where this animal lives.

STUDY AND COMPARE THESE TWO BEACHES

Beach #1 Tiwi Beach, Kenya

Beach #2 Panama City Beach, Florida, USA.

Contact the local wildlife society or nature center to learn more!

DRAW 2 SHELLS THAT CAN BE FOUND ON EACH BEACH.

Beach #1   Beach #2

LIST 4 LAND ANIMALS THAT CAN BE FOUND AT EACH BEACH

LIST 4 SEA CREATURES THAT CAN BE FOUND NEAR THIS BEACH

LIST 4 BIRDS THAT CAN BE SPOTTED NEAR THIS BEACH

COLOR AND RESEARCH
EACH OF THESE REALISTIC DRAWINGS

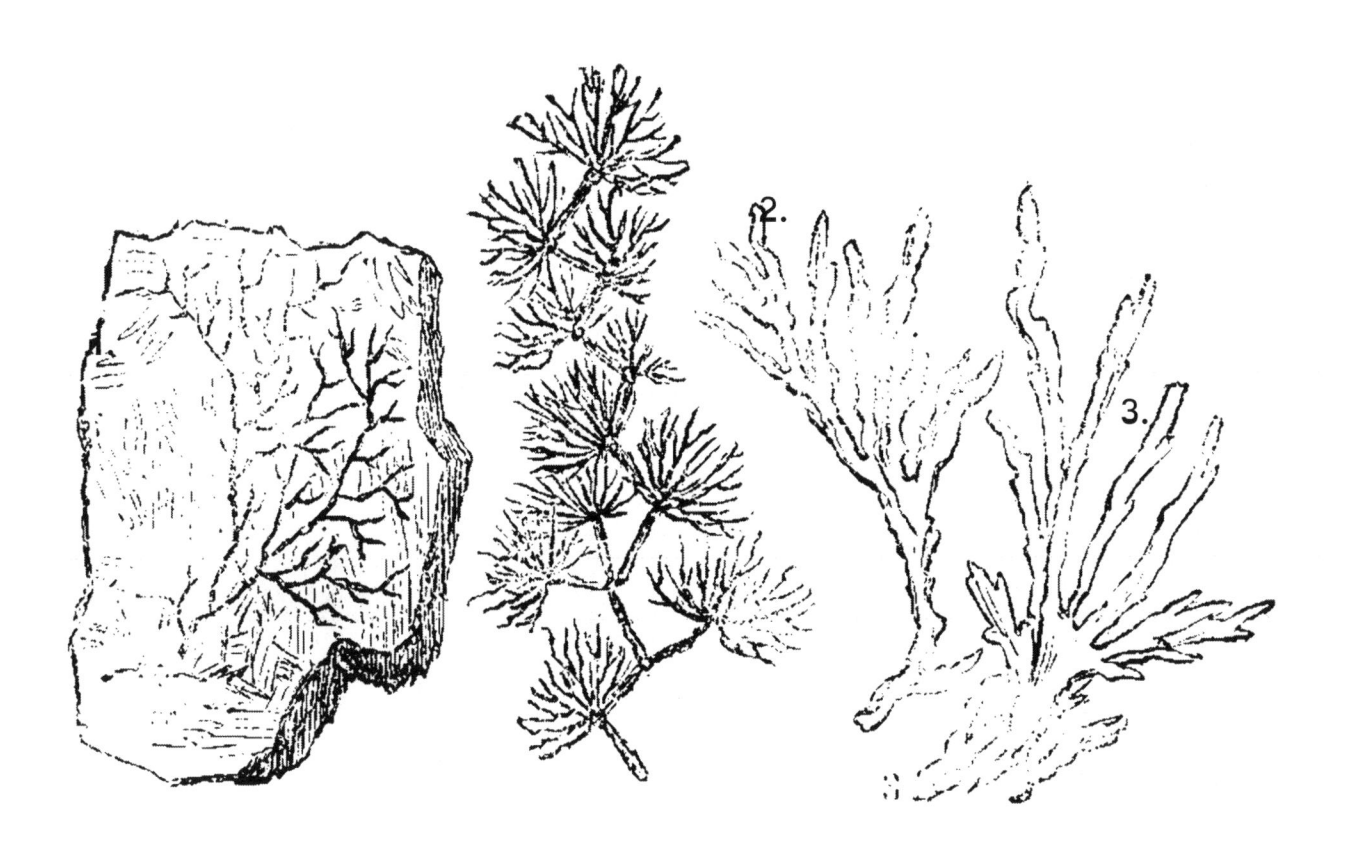

1. Petrifaction Chondrite. 2. Murchisonites Forbesi. 3. Ancient Chondrites.

DRAW TWO OF YOUR FAVORITES WITH A FINE POINT BLACK PEN.

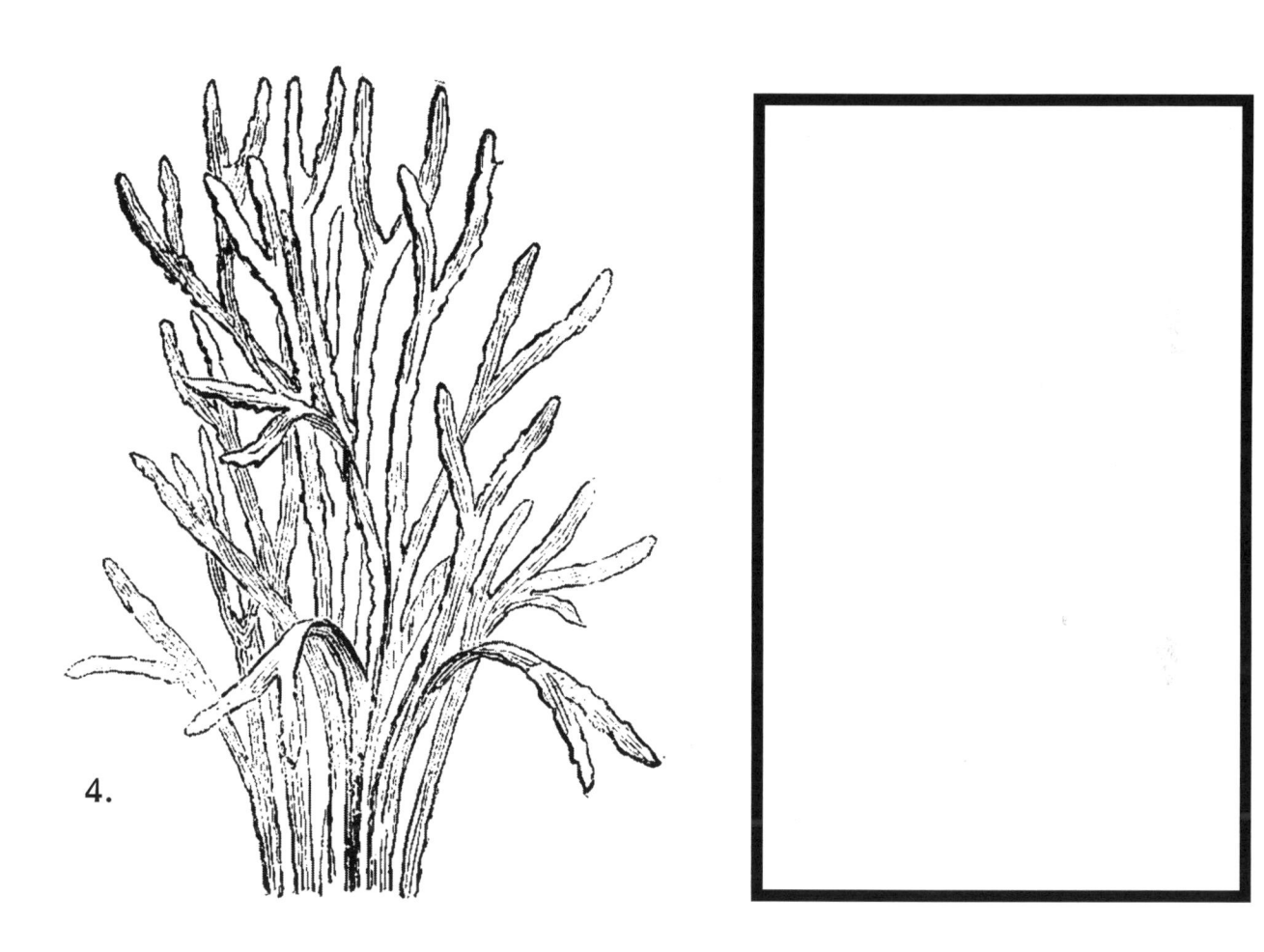

4.

4. Seaweed

169

1. COLOR

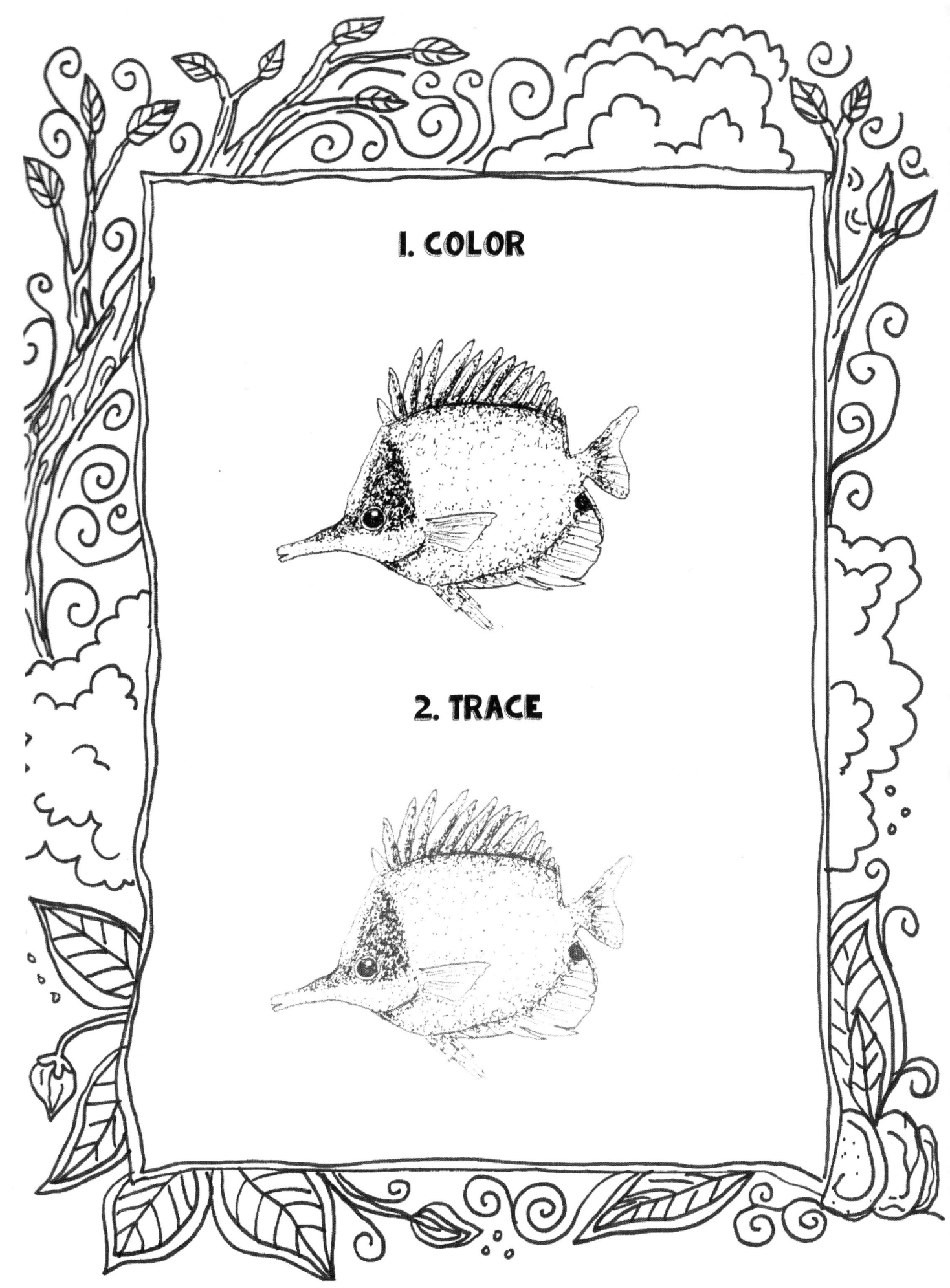

2. TRACE

3. DRAW THE MISSING PART:

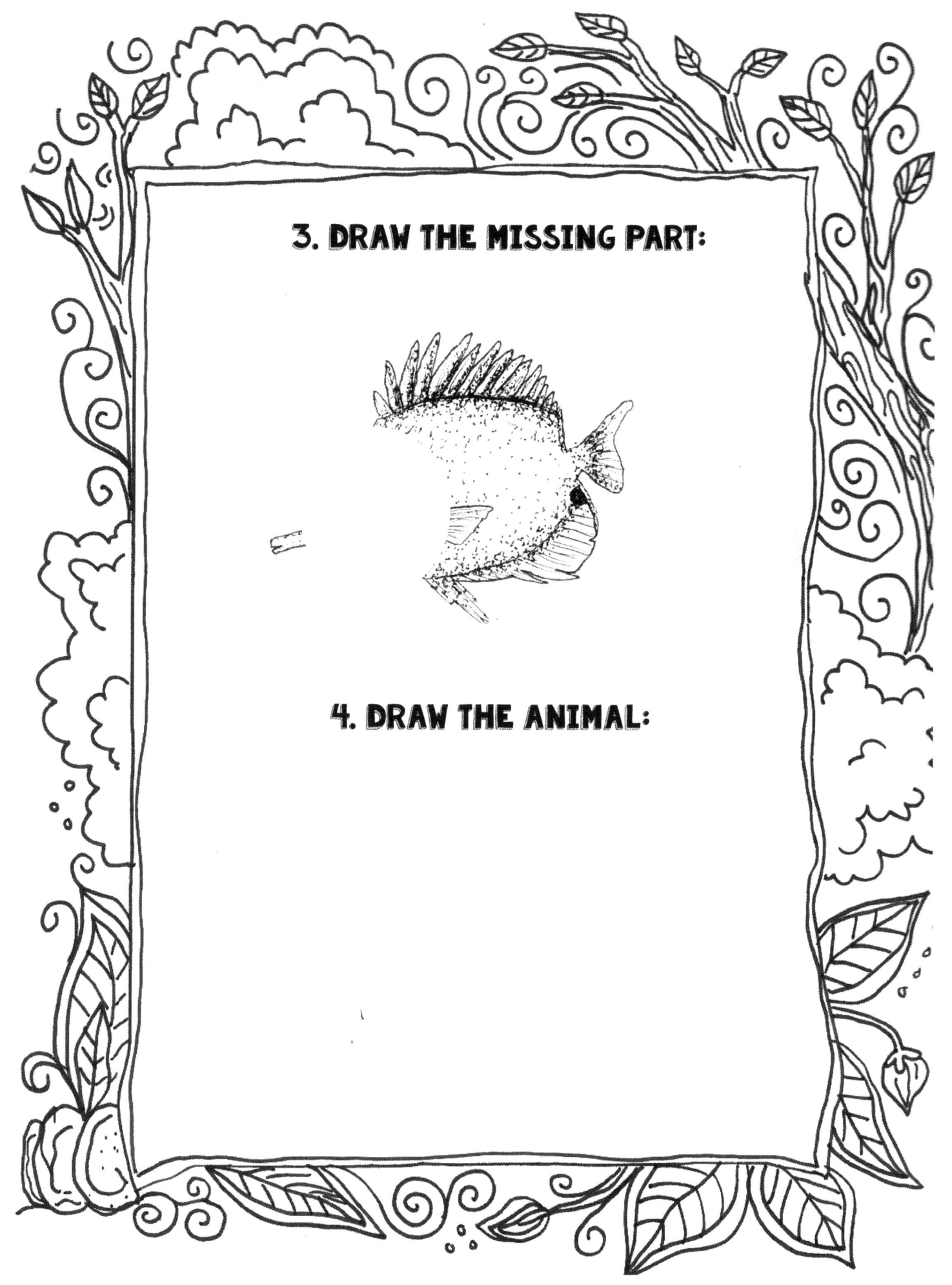

4. DRAW THE ANIMAL:

Choose a book from your nature library to read today. Document your learning with words and pictures here!

Today's Date:

READING TIME

COLOR ME
DRAW MY FOOD & HABITAT

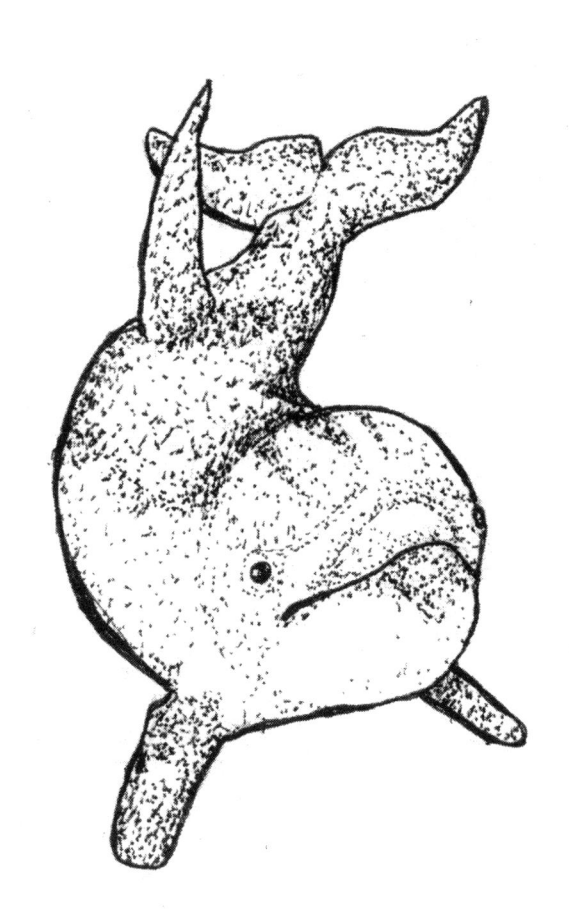

COMMON NAME:
Protea

What is the Scientific Name:

_____

RESEARCH THIS PLANT

What can this plant be used for?

_____   _____
_____   _____
_____   _____

Where did it originate?

_____
_____

Where else can it be found?

_____
_____

How did it travel to other parts of the world?

_____
_____

Is this plant in danger of extinction? Why or Why Not?

_____
_____

ANIMALS IN MY REGION

What animal are you learning about?

Common Name:_____

Scientific Name:_____

Draw a Male

Draw a Female

Color the other parts of the world where this animal lives.

COLOR AND RESEARCH EACH OF THESE REALISTIC DRAWINGS

1.

2.

3.

4.

5.

1. Shark   2 & 3. Jellyfish   4. Crab   5. Sea Horse

DRAW TWO OF YOUR FAVORITES WITH A FINE POINT BLACK PEN.

6.

7.

8.

6. Sea Turtle 7. Teardrop Butterfly 8. Moorish Idol

STUDY AND COMPARE THESE TWO BEACHES

Beach #1 Tulum, Mexico

Beach #2 Edisto Beach, South Carolina, USA.

Contact the local wildlife society or nature center to learn more!

DRAW 2 SHELLS THAT CAN BE FOUND ON EACH BEACH.

Beach #1   Beach #2

LIST 4 LAND ANIMALS THAT CAN BE FOUND AT EACH BEACH

_____   _____
_____   _____
_____   _____
_____   _____

LIST 4 SEA CREATURES THAT CAN BE FOUND NEAR THIS BEACH

_____   _____
_____   _____
_____   _____
_____   _____

LIST 4 BIRDS THAT CAN BE SPOTTED NEAR THIS BEACH

_____   _____
_____   _____
_____   _____
_____   _____

NATURE NOTES, QUOTES AND POETRY

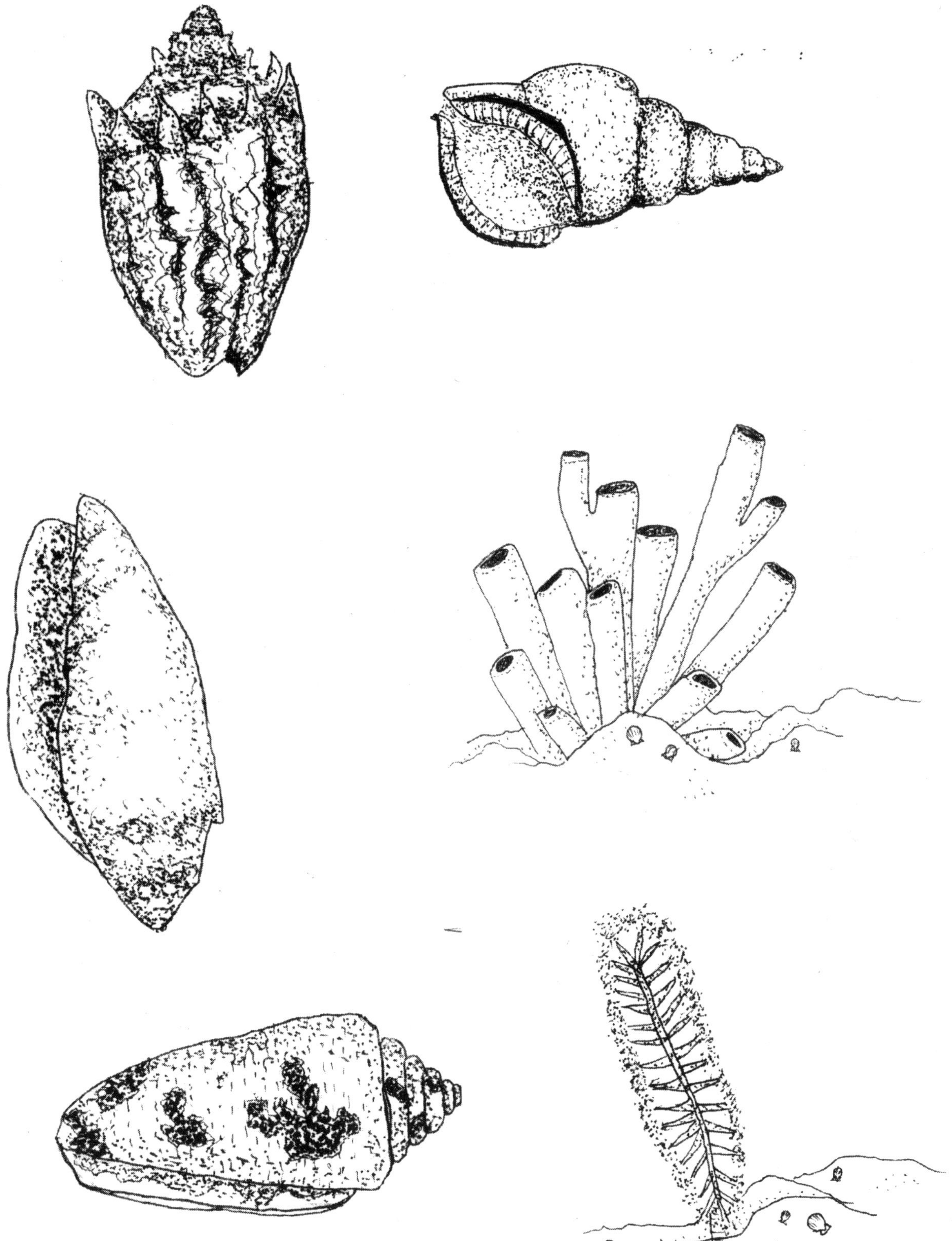

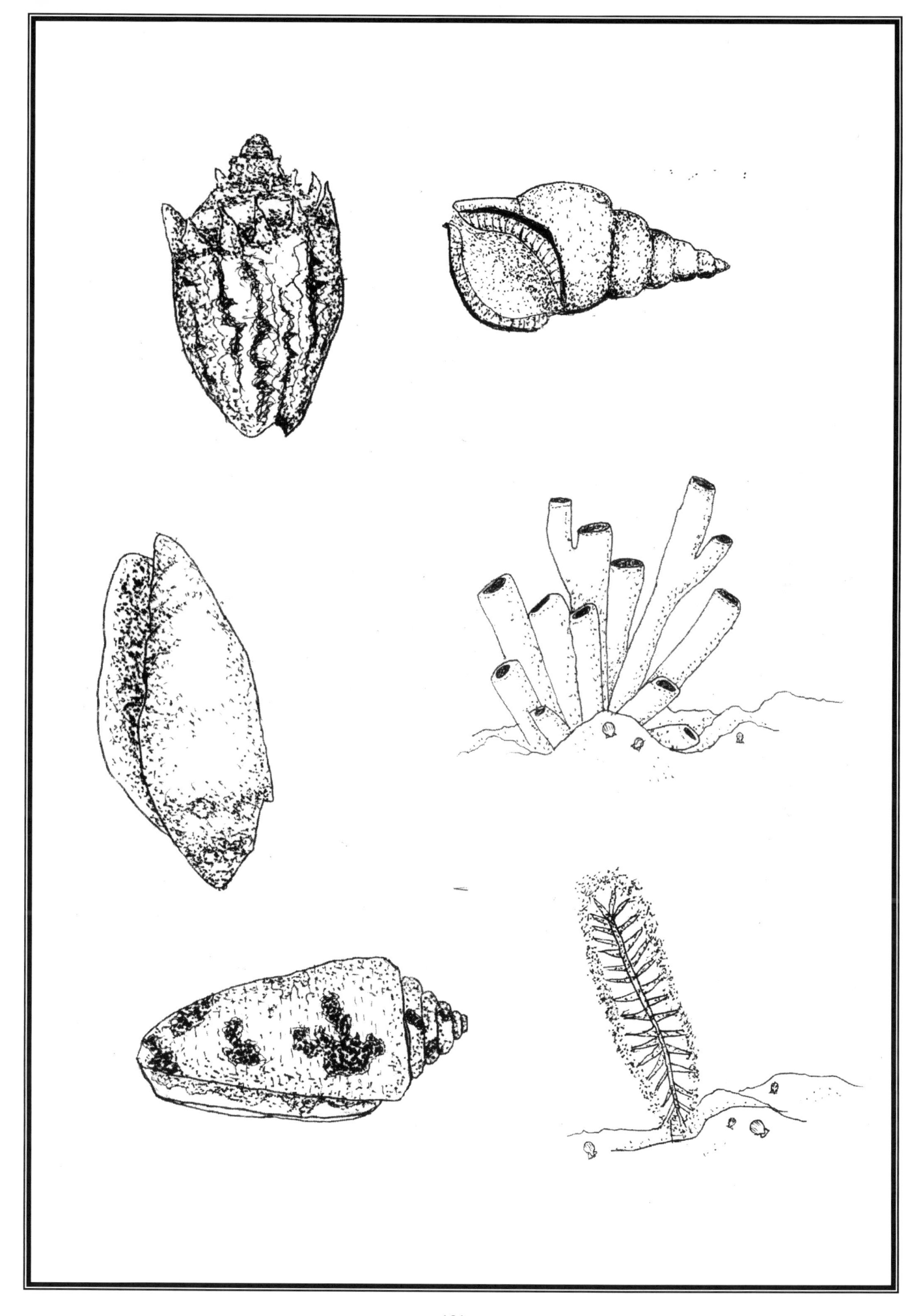

COLLECT 10 SMALL THINGS FROM NATURE AND MAKE A NATURE CRAFT.

DRAW SMALL THINGS YOU SEE OUTSIDE

COMMON NAME:

Monstera

What is the Scientific Name:

_____

RESEARCH THIS PLANT

What can this plant be used for?

_____ _____
_____ _____
_____ _____

Where did it originate?

_____
_____

Where else can it be found?

_____
_____

How did it travel to other parts of the world?

_____
_____

Is this plant in danger of extinction? Why or Why Not?

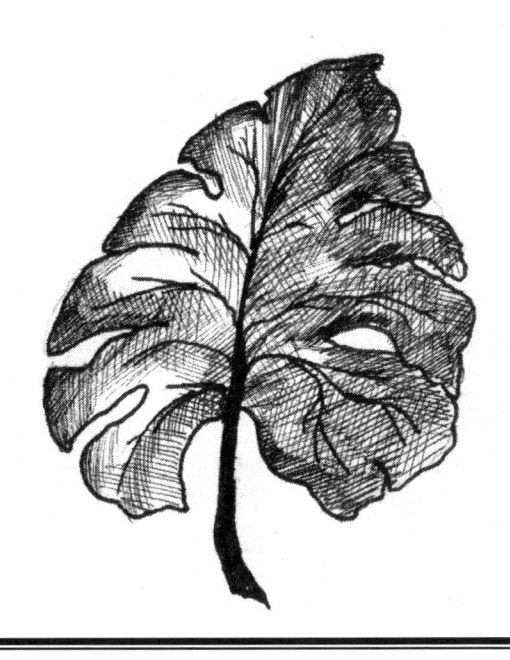

_____
_____

ANIMALS IN MY REGION

What animal are you learning about?

Common Name:_____

Scientific Name:_____

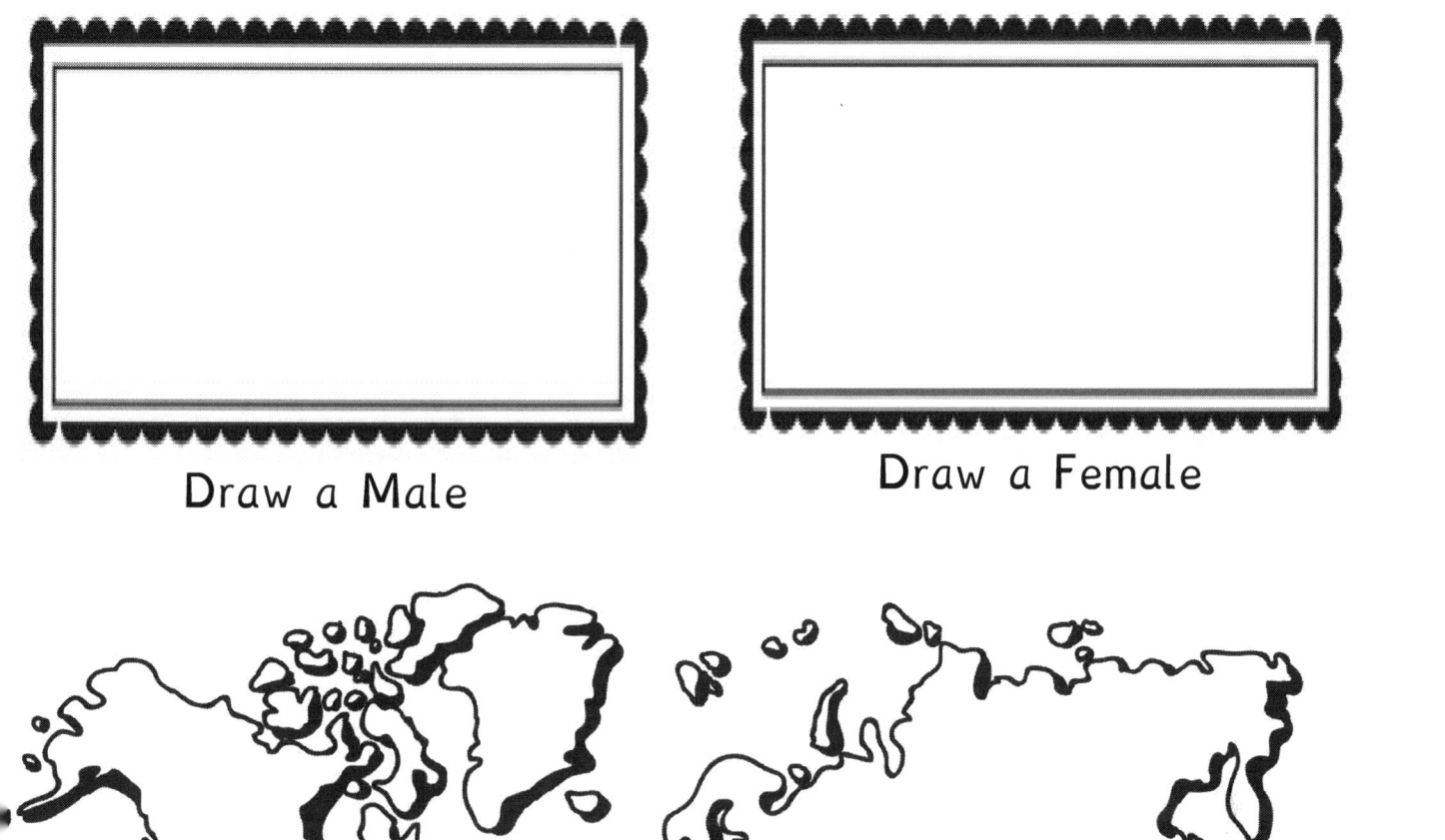

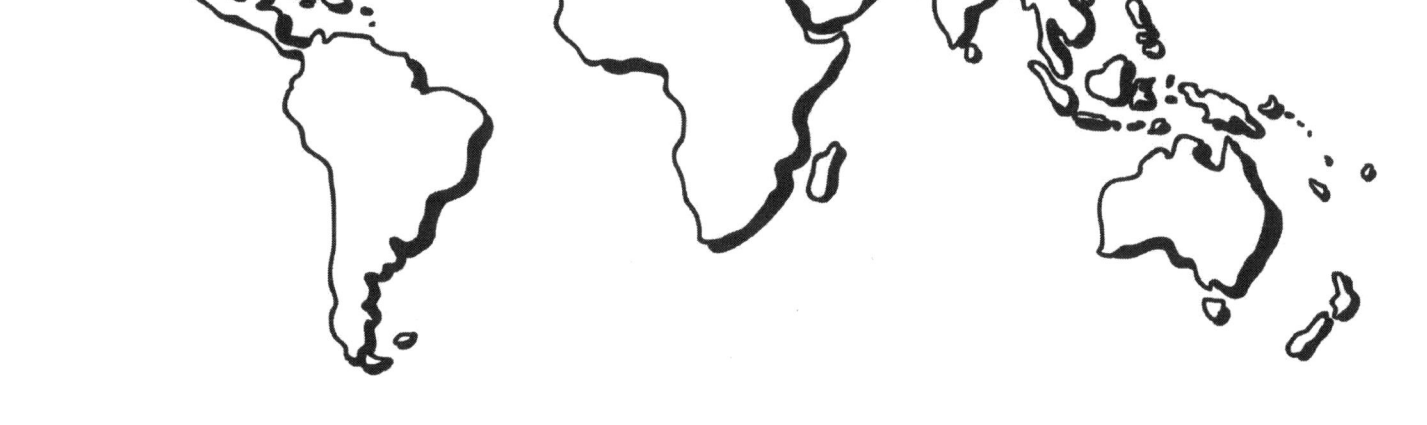

Draw a Male

Draw a Female

Color the other parts of the world where this animal lives.

COLOR AND RESEARCH
EACH OF THESE REALISTIC DRAWINGS

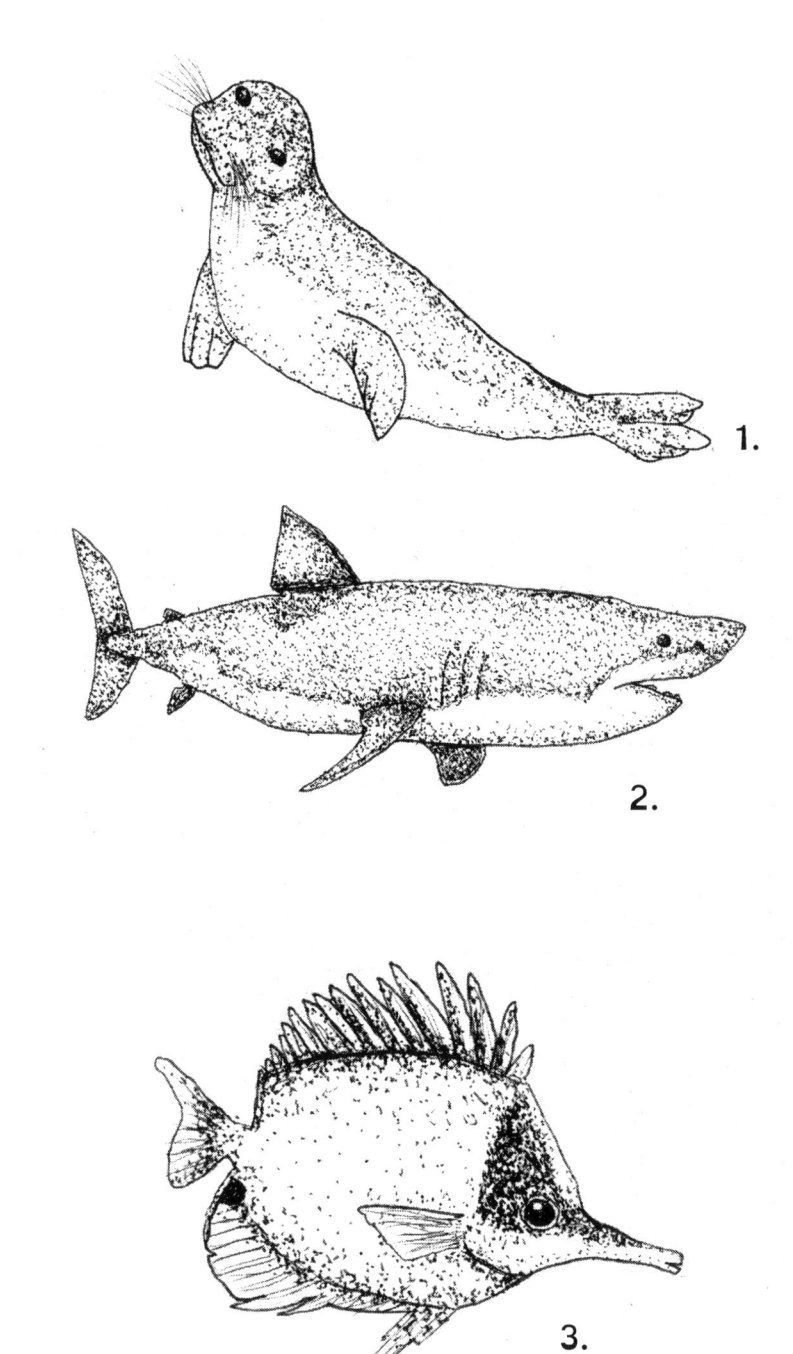

1.

2.

3.

1. Hawaiian Monk Seal   2. White Shark   3. The Yellow Longnose Butterflyfish

DRAW TWO OF YOUR FAVORITES WITH A FINE POINT BLACK PEN.

4.

5.

4. Dolphin 5. Whale

STUDY AND COMPARE THESE TWO BEACHES

Beach #1 Odessa, Ukraine

Beach #2 Gulf Coast of Alabama, USA.

Contact the local wildlife society or nature center to learn more!

DRAW 2 SHELLS THAT CAN BE FOUND ON EACH BEACH.

Beach #1   Beach #2

LIST 4 LAND ANIMALS THAT CAN BE FOUND AT EACH BEACH

_____   _____
_____   _____
_____   _____
_____   _____

LIST 4 SEA CREATURES THAT CAN BE FOUND NEAR THIS BEACH

_____   _____
_____   _____
_____   _____
_____   _____

LIST 4 BIRDS THAT CAN BE SPOTTED NEAR THIS BEACH

_____   _____
_____   _____
_____   _____
_____   _____

Choose a book from your nature library to read today. Document your learning with words and pictures here!

READING TIME

Today's Date: _____

DRAW A PICTURE FROM ONE OF YOUR NATURE BOOKS ABOUT JELLYFISH

**PLAN A HIKE OR CAMPING TRIP
DRAW EVERYTHING YOU WILL TAKE WITH YOU**

LOOK IN A BOOK & DRAW A FRUIT IN EACH BOX

LOOK IN A BOOK & DRAW A SPIDER IN EACH BOX

COMMON NAME:
Needle Palm

What is the Scientific Name:

RESEARCH THIS PLANT

What can this plant be used for?

------------------------   ------------------------------
------------------------   ------------------------------
------------------------   ------------------------------

Where did it originate?

Where else can it be found?

How did it travel to other parts of the world?

Is this plant in danger of extinction? Why or Why Not?

ANIMALS IN MY REGION

What animal are you learning about?
Common Name:_____
Scientific Name:_____

Draw a Male

Draw a Female

Color the other parts of the world where this animal lives.

Choose a book from your nature library to read today. Document your learning with words and pictures here!

READING TIME

Today's Date:

COLOR ME
DRAW MY FOOD & HABITAT

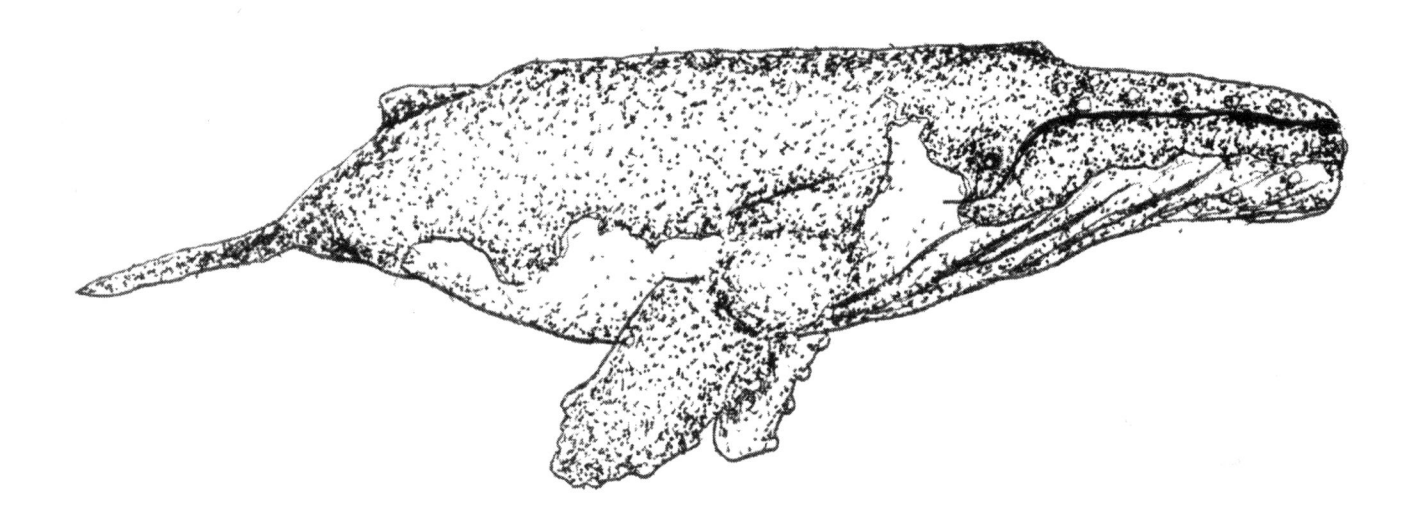

COLOR AND RESEARCH EACH OF THESE REALISTIC DRAWINGS

1.

2.

3.

4.

1. Red-crested Cardinal 2. Red-footed Booby 3. Red Junglefowl

DRAW TWO OF YOUR FAVORITES WITH A FINE POINT BLACK PEN.

5.

4. Java Sparrow   5. Nene Goose

201

STUDY AND COMPARE THESE TWO BEACHES

Beach #1 Point Beach on Cape Cod, Provincetown, Massachusetts, USA

Beach #2 Na Pali Coast on Kauai, USA.

Contact the local wildlife society or nature center to learn more!

DRAW 2 SHELLS THAT CAN BE FOUND ON EACH BEACH.

Beach #1   Beach #2

LIST 4 LAND ANIMALS THAT CAN BE FOUND AT EACH BEACH

LIST 4 SEA CREATURES THAT CAN BE FOUND NEAR THIS BEACH

LIST 4 BIRDS THAT CAN BE SPOTTED NEAR THIS BEACH

DRAW A PICTURE OF YOUR FAVORITE SEA BIRD

RESEARCH YOUR FAVORITE SEA BIRD

1. COLOR

2. TRACE

3. DRAW THE MISSING PART:

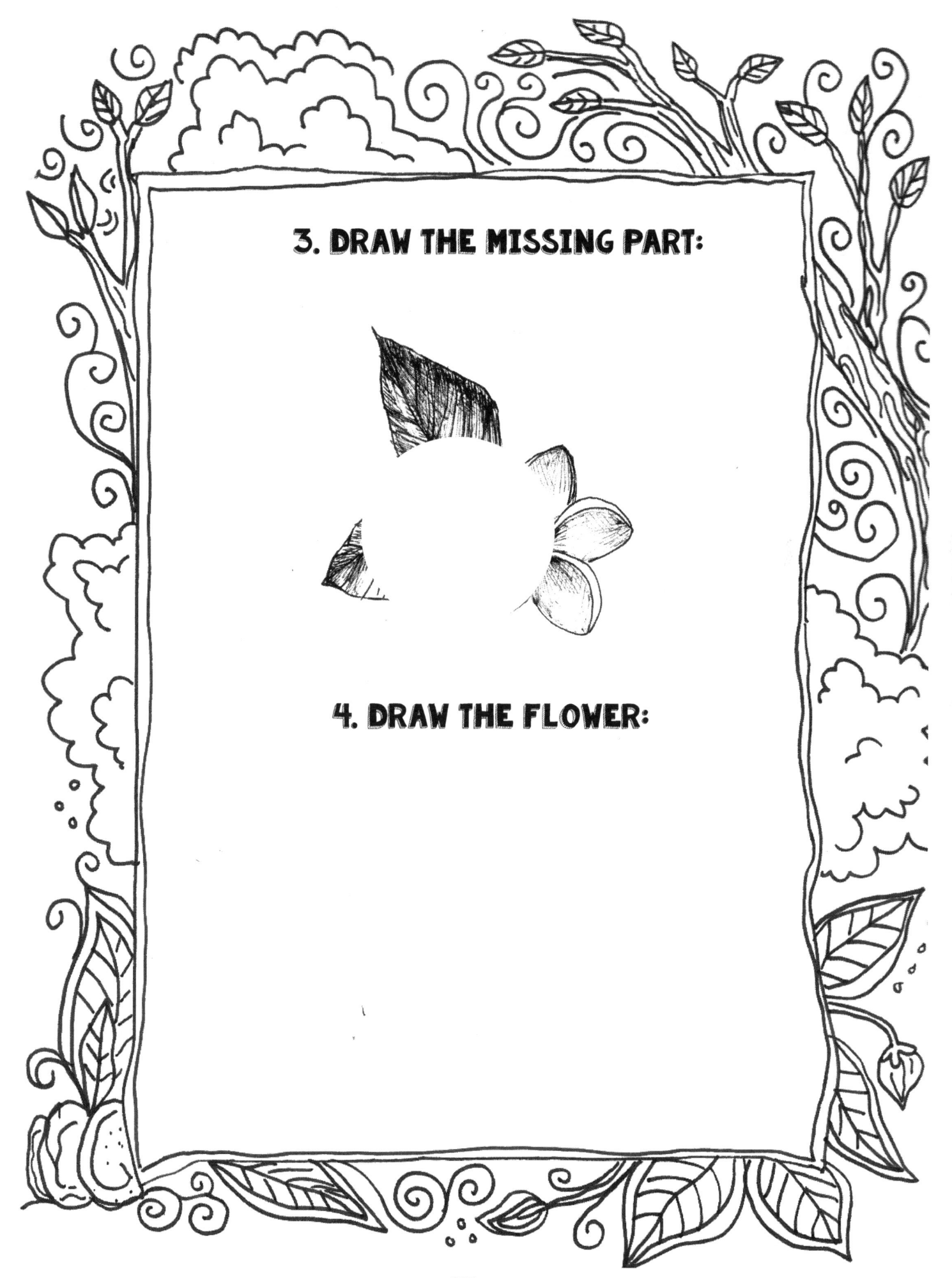

4. DRAW THE FLOWER:

Choose a book from your nature library to read today. Document your learning with words and pictures here!

Today's Date:

READING TIME

COLOR ME
DRAW MY FOOD & HABITAT

GO OUTSIDE AND DRAW A LEAF IN EACH BOX

FIND AND COLOR IN THE HIDDEN OBJECTS

COMMON NAME:
Banana Leaf

What is the Scientific Name:

_____

RESEARCH THIS PLANT

What can this plant be used for?

_____ _____
_____ _____
_____ _____

Where did it originate?
_____
_____

Where else can it be found?
_____
_____

How did it travel to other parts of the world?
_____
_____

Is this plant in danger of extinction? Why or Why Not?
_____
_____

ANIMALS IN MY REGION

What animal are you learning about?

Common Name:_____

Scientific Name:_____

Draw a Male

Draw a Female

Color the other parts of the world where this animal lives.

STUDY AND COMPARE THESE TWO BEACHES

Beach #1 Point Chesapeake Bay in Maryland, USA

Beach #2 Outer Banks of North Carolina, USA.

Contact the local wildlife society or nature center to learn more!

DRAW 2 SHELLS THAT CAN BE FOUND ON EACH BEACH.

Beach #1   Beach #2

LIST 4 LAND ANIMALS THAT CAN BE FOUND AT EACH BEACH

_____   _____
_____   _____
_____   _____
_____   _____

LIST 4 SEA CREATURES THAT CAN BE FOUND NEAR THIS BEACH

_____   _____
_____   _____
_____   _____
_____   _____

LIST 4 BIRDS THAT CAN BE SPOTTED NEAR THIS BEACH

_____   _____
_____   _____
_____   _____
_____   _____

GO ON A HIKE OR NATURE WALK AND DRAW WHAT YOU SEE.

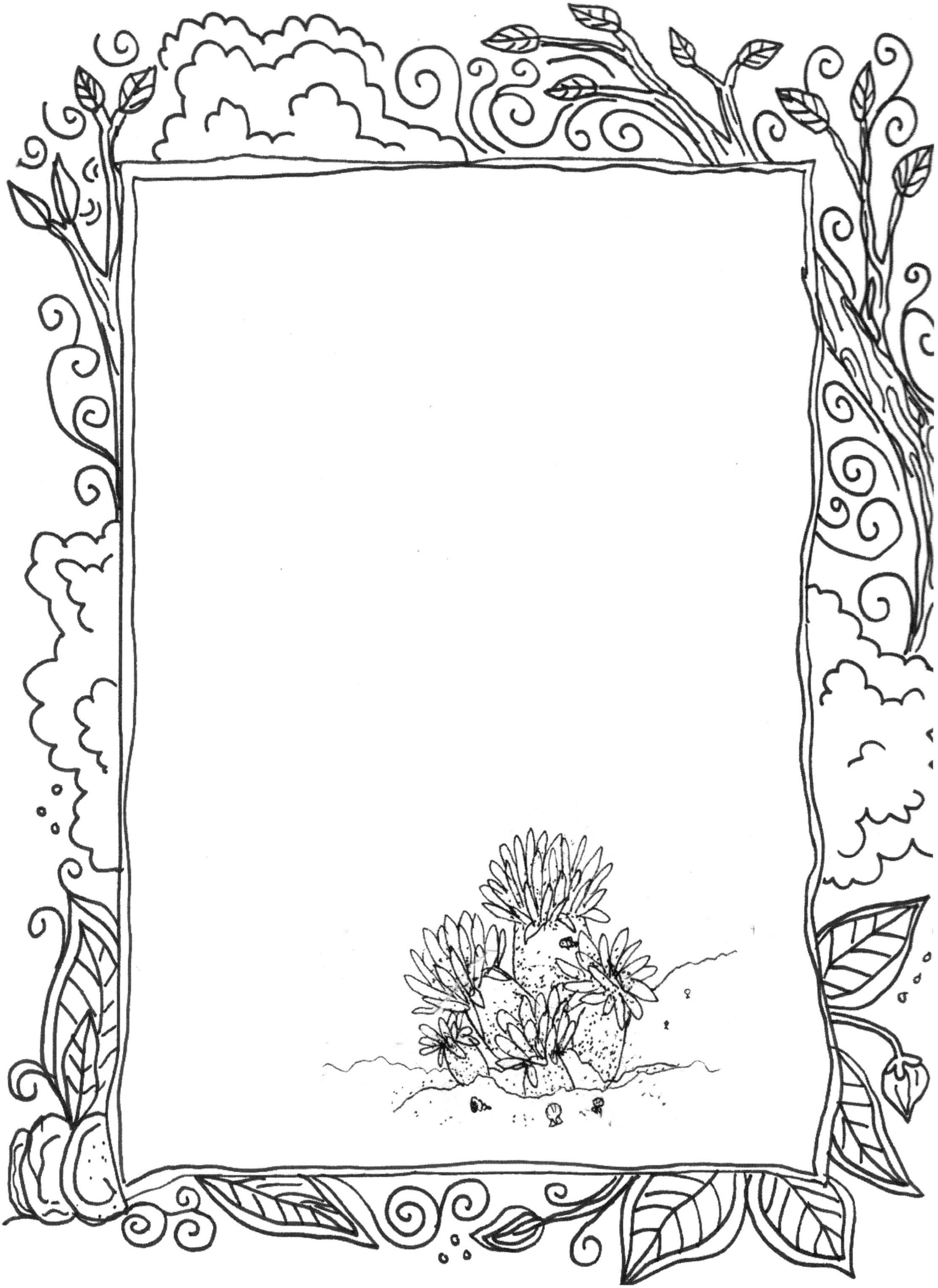

1. COLOR

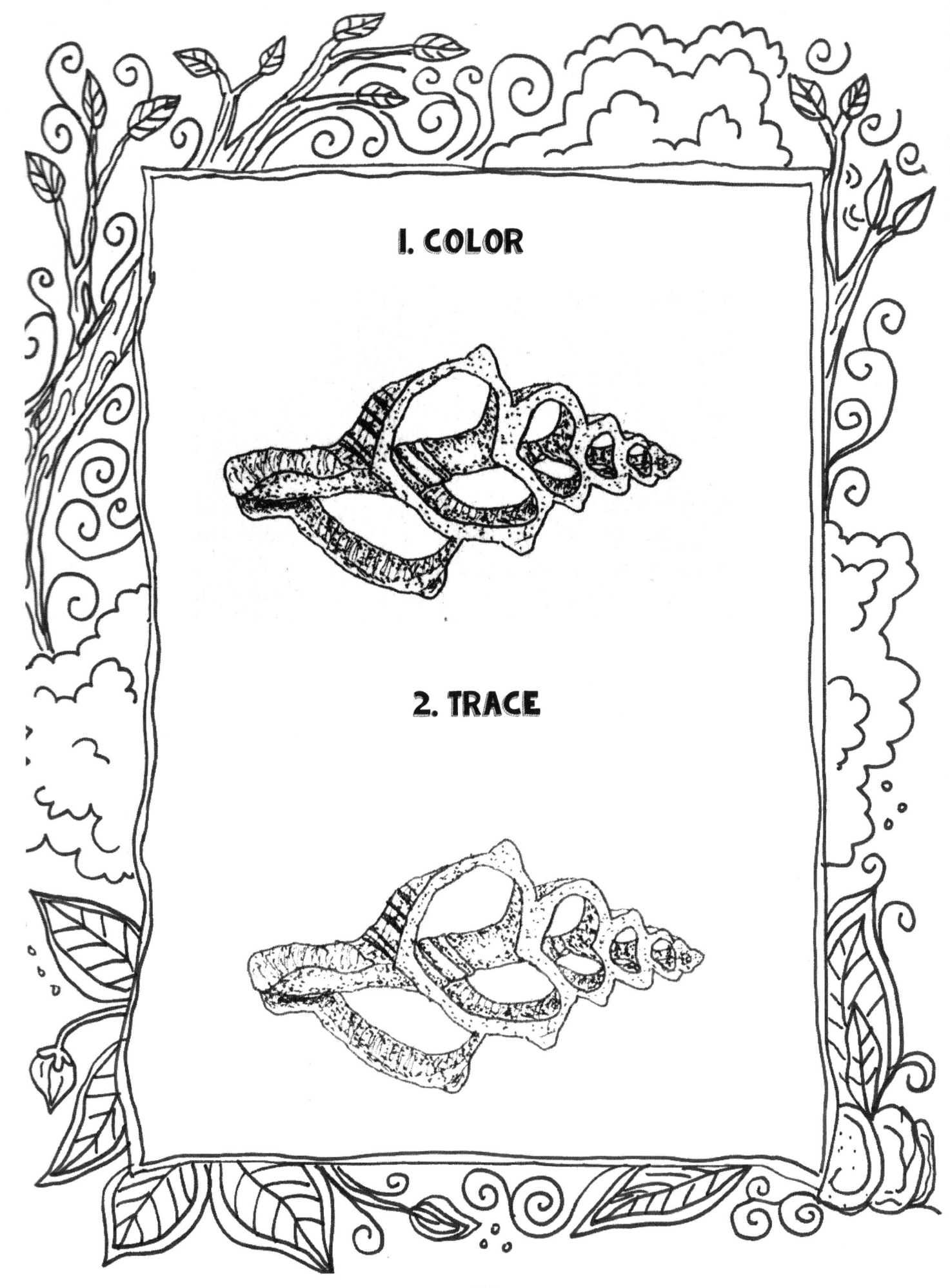

2. TRACE

3. DRAW THE MISSING PART:

4. DRAW THE SHELL:

RESEARCH SOMETHING YOU SEE OUTSIDE TODAY.

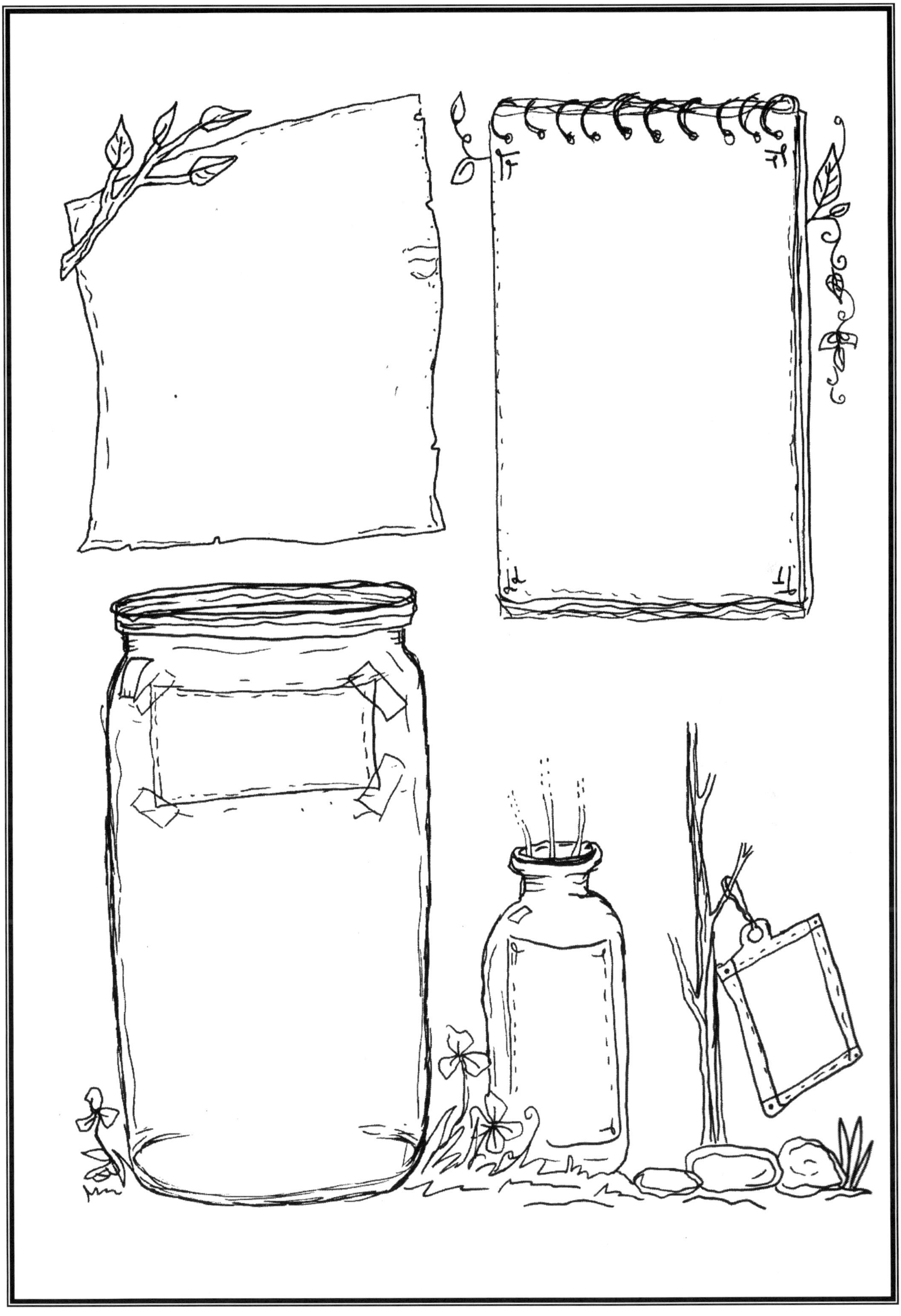

Choose a book from your nature library to read today. Document your learning with words and pictures here!

Today's Date:

READING TIME

FIND AND COLOR IN THE HIDDEN OBJECTS

COMMON NAME:
Fern

What is the Scientific Name:

_____

RESEARCH THIS PLANT

What can this plant be used for?

_____ _____
_____ _____
_____ _____

Where did it originate?

_____
_____

Where else can it be found?

_____
_____

How did it travel to other parts of the world?

_____
_____

Is this plant in danger of extinction? Why or Why Not?

_____
_____

ANIMALS IN MY REGION

What animal are you learning about?

Common Name:_____

Scientific Name:_____

Draw a Male

Draw a Female

Color the other parts of the world where this animal lives.

STUDY AND COMPARE THESE TWO BEACHES

Beach #1 Laguna Beach, California, USA

Beach #2 The coast of Newport Rhode Island, USA.

Contact the local wildlife society or nature center to learn more!

DRAW 2 SHELLS THAT CAN BE FOUND ON EACH BEACH.

Beach #1　　　　　　　　　　　　　　　Beach #2

LIST 4 LAND ANIMALS THAT CAN BE FOUND AT EACH BEACH

_____　　_____
_____　　_____
_____　　_____
_____　　_____

LIST 4 SEA CREATURES THAT CAN BE FOUND NEAR THIS BEACH

_____　　_____
_____　　_____
_____　　_____
_____　　_____

LIST 4 BIRDS THAT CAN BE SPOTTED NEAR THIS BEACH

_____　　_____
_____　　_____
_____　　_____
_____　　_____

228

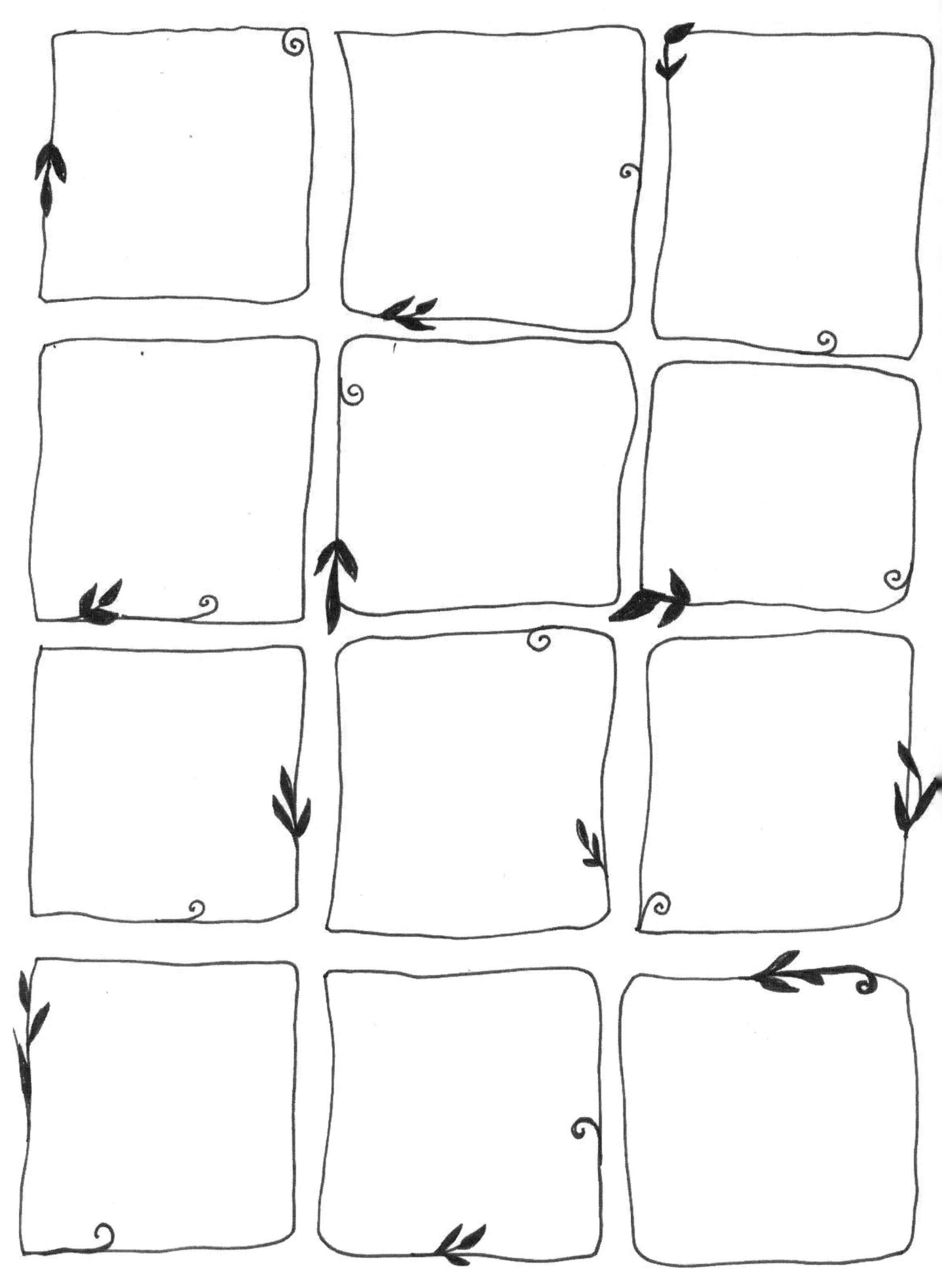

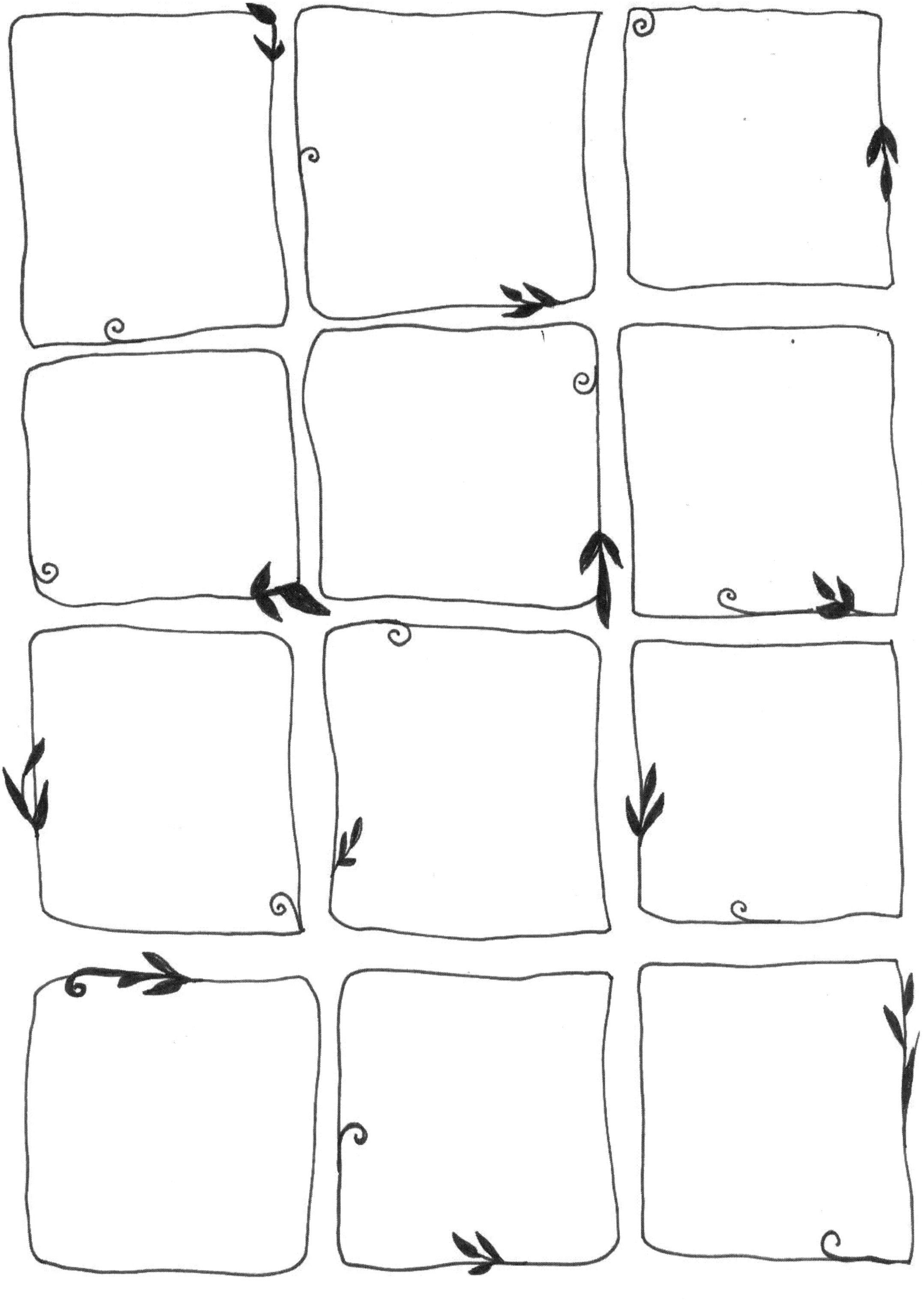

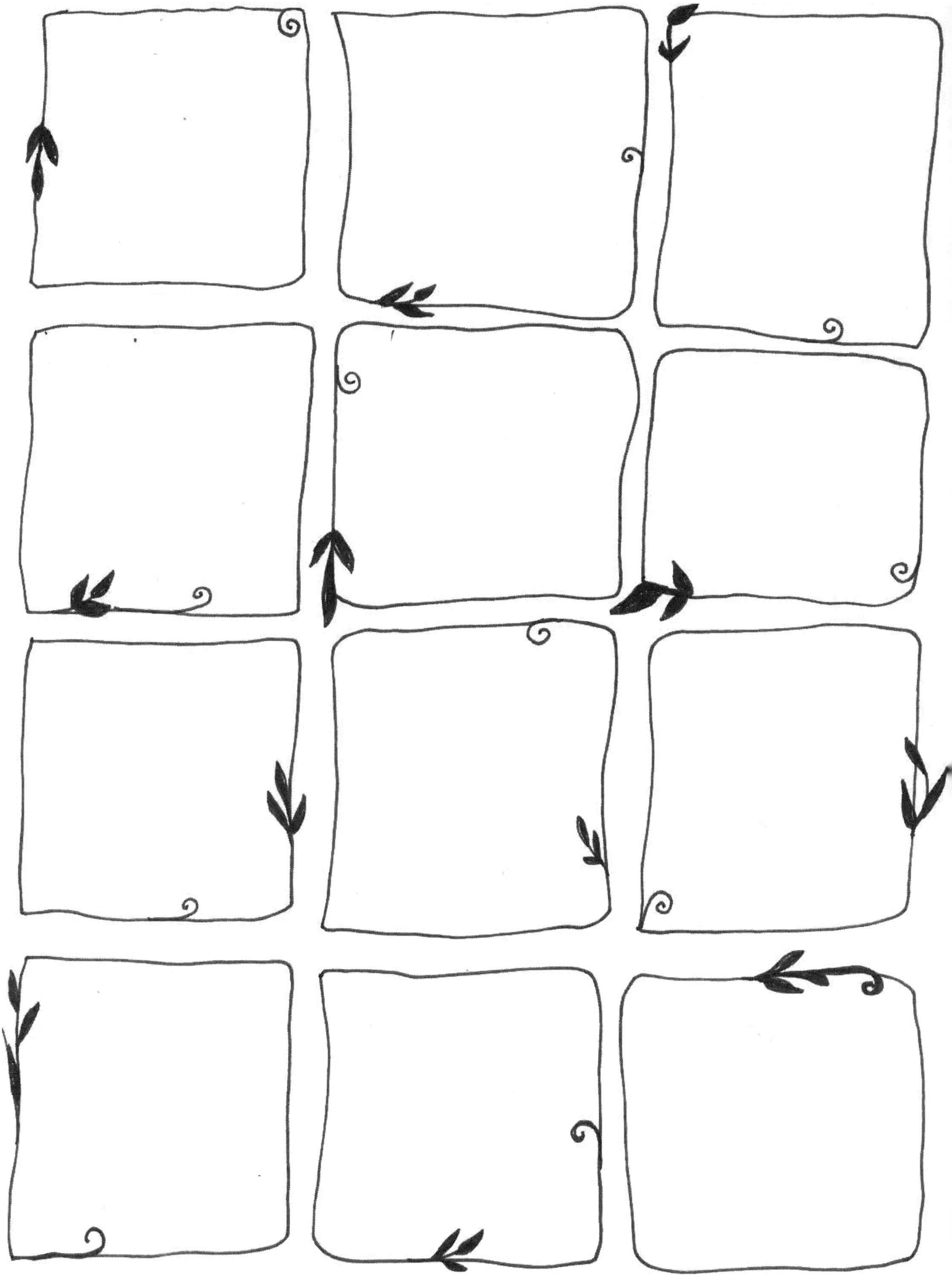

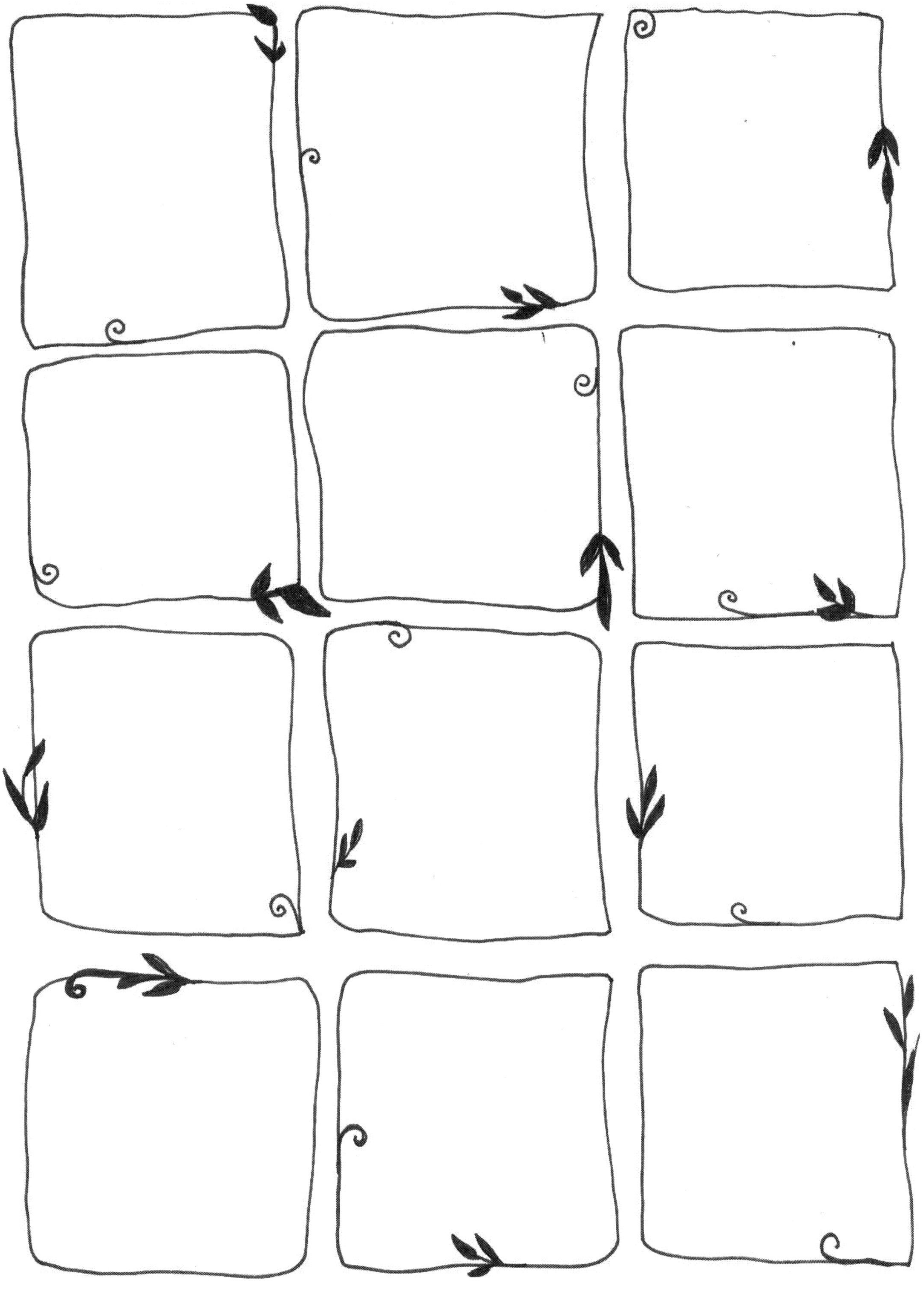

The Thinking Tree

FunSchoolingBooks.com

Made in the USA
Columbia, SC
12 June 2025